WRITERS AND THEIR WORK

ISOBEL ARMSTRONG
Consultant Editor

GEORGE MEREDITH

GEORGE MEREDITH

Jacqueline Banerjee

For My Husband

© Copyright 2012 by Jacqueline Banerjee

First published by Northcote House Publishers Ltd, Horndon House, Horndon, Tavistock, Devon, PL19 9NQ, United Kingdom.
Tel: +44 (0) 1822 810066 Fax: +44 (0) 1822 810034.

All rights reserved. No part of this work may be reproduced or stored in an information retrieval system (other than short extracts for the purposes of review) without the express permission of the Publishers given in writing.

British Library Cataloguing-in-Publication Data
A catalogue record for this book is available from the British Library

ISBN 978-0-7463-1213-1 hardcover
ISBN 978-0-7463-1214-8 paperback

Typeset by PDQ Typesetting, Newcastle-under-Lyme
Printed and bound in the United Kingdom

Contents

List of Illustrations   vi
Biographical Outline   vii
Abbreviations and References   xi
Introduction   1
1   A Life in Stages   5
2   *Poems* (1851) and 'Modern Love'   22
3   The First 'Thwackings': From *The Shaving of Shagpat* to *The Adventures of Harry Richmond*   39
4   A New Kind of Hero: From *Beauchamp's Career* to *The Egoist*   59
5   The Later Novels: Meredith as Feminist?   76
6   The Later Poetry   91
Notes   101
Select Bibliography   113
Index   122

Illustrations

Frontispiece

Thomas Love Peacock's Thames-side house on
Lower Halliford Green   8

The beleaguered writer and his young sympathizer, as
illustrated by E.H. Wehnert in *The Magic Words: A Tale
for Christmas Time*   12

Millais' illustration for 'The Meeting', a short lyric
published in *Once a Week* in September 1862   15

Meredith's writing chalet on the lower slopes of Box Hill   18

Vine Cottage on Lower Halliford Green   31

Meredith and Arthur, his son by Mary Ellen, in a
photograph taken by William Hardman in 1862   42

Emilie Maceroni (later Lady Hornby), the original of
Emilia Sandra Belloni (Vittoria)   51

An illustration by George du Maurier in *Harry Richmond*   57

Frederick Maxse   60

Crossways Farm   80

'The Druid's Grove, Norbury Park: Ancient Yew Trees'
by Thomas Allom   92

'George Meredith aet 72', from a dry-point etching
by Mortimer Menpes   98

Biographical Outline

1828	George Meredith born on 12 February, to Augustus Meredith, tailor and naval outfitter, and his wife Jane (née Macnamara), of 73 High Street, Portsmouth; grandmother dies in November.
1833	Mother dies in July.
1837	Enters St Paul's School, Southsea.
1838	Father's business fails.
1839	Father moves to London and remarries; removes George from St Paul's, and leaves him with relatives near Petersfield.
1842	Enrolled in the Morovian School at Neuwied, near Cologne, on 18 August.
1844	Returns to England on 7 January.
1846	Articled on 3 February to Richard Charnock, a solicitor. Gets to know the son and daughter of Thomas Love Peacock.
1849	Marries Mary Ellen Nicolls, Peacock's widowed daughter, on 9 August, at St George's, Hanover Square.
1851	*Poems*, dedicated to Peacock, published by Peacock's friend J. W. Parker.
1853	First son (only child by Mary Ellen), Arthur Gryffydh Meredith, born on 13 June.
1855	*The Shaving of Shagpat: An Arabian Entertainment* published by Chapman & Hall.
1857	*Farina: A Legend of Cologne* published by Smith, Elder.
1858	Mary Ellen Meredith spends several months on Capri with the artist Henry Wallis, having earlier borne him a son, Harold.
1859	*The Ordeal of Richard Feverel* published by Chapman & Hall.
1860	*Evan Harrington* appears serially in *Once a Week*,

BIOGRAPHICAL OUTLINE

	February–October. Appointed reader for Chapman & Hall publishers.
1861	*Evan Harrington* published by Harper & Bros. Taking Arthur, travels through the Continent during July and August with his friend Bonaparte Wyse. Mary Ellen Meredith dies of kidney disease in October.
1862	*Modern Love and Poems of the English Roadside* published by Chapman & Hall.
1863	Another Continental walking trip, late August and September, this time with Lionel Robinson.
1864	*Emilia in England* published by Chapman & Hall (retitled *Sandra Belloni* in 1886). Marries Marie Vulliamy, 20 September, at St Michael and All Angels, Mickleham, Surrey.
1865	Second son, William Maxse Meredith, born at Kingston Lodge, Kingston, Surrey, on 27 July. *Rhoda Fleming* published by Tinsley Brothers.
1866	*Vittoria* serialized in *The Fortnightly Review*, January–December. In Italy as a war correspondent, June–July. Revised version of *Vittoria* published by Chapman & Hall at the end of the year. Now acting as Editor of *The Fortnightly Review*.
1868	Moves to Flint Cottage on Box Hill, near Dorking, Surrey.
1870	*The Adventures of Harry Richmond* appears serially in *The Cornhill Magazine* from September until April 1871.
1871	'France, December 1870' published in the *Fortnightly Review* in January. Only daughter, Marie (Mariette, or Riette) Meredith, born on 9 June. *The Adventures of Harry Richmond* published by Smith, Elder in October; second edition brought out by the end of the year.
1874	*Beauchamp's Career* serialized in *The Fortnightly Review*, from August to December 1875.
1876	*Beauchamp's Career* published by Chapman & Hall.
1877	'The House on the Beach' published in *The New Quarterly Magazine* in January. Gives talk 'On the Idea of Comedy and the Uses of the Comic Spirit' on 1 February at the London Institution; talk published in *The New Quarterly* in April. 'The Case of General Ople and Lady Camper' published in *The New Quarterly* in July.

1879	*The Egoist* published by Kegan Paul; also serialized in *The Glasgow Herald* as *Sir Willoughby Patterne: The Egoist* from June until January 1880. 'The Tale of Chloe' published in *The New Quarterly* in July.
1880	Abridged version of *The Tragic Comedians: A Study in a Well-Known Story* serialized in the *Fortnightly Review* from October onwards; published by Chapman & Hall in December.
1883	*Poems and Lyrics of the Joy of Earth* published by Macmillan. Beginning of the Sunday Tramps, led by Leslie Stephen.
1884	*Diana of the Crossways* appears serially in *The Fortnightly Review* from June to December, only reaching Chapter 26.
1885	*Diana of the Crossways* published by Chapman & Hall; two more editions published.
1886	Second wife Marie dies of cancer, 18 September. Eight-volume uniform edition of his works (2,000 copies of each) published by Chapman & Hall.
1887	Article on Meredith by Flora Shaw in *The Princeton Review* for March. *Ballads and Poems of Tragic Life* published.
1888	*A Reading of Earth* (poems) published.
1890	Son Arthur dies of consumption, 3 September. *One of Our Conquerors* serialized in *The Fortnightly Review* and *The Australasian*, January to October.
1891	*One of Our Conquerors* serialized in *The New York Sun*, January to May, and published in a 3-volume edition by Chapman & Hall.
1892	First of three gallstone operations in June. Elected President of the Society of Authors this autumn. Son William marries Daisy Elliot, 4 October. *The Empty Purse* (poems) published in October by Macmillan.
1893	*Lord Ormont and His Aminta* serialized in *Pall Mall Magazine* from December (to July 1894).
1894	Fuller version of *Lord Ormont and His Aminta* published by Chapman & Hall in June. Meredith resigns from Chapman & Hall. Daughter marries Henry Parkman Sturgis, a businessman living in nearby Leatherhead, 17 July.

1895	*The Amazing Marriage* appears serially in *Scribner's Magazine,* January to December.
1896	Attends last public function (Private View of the New Gallery Exhibition, London) in April. Constable starts bringing out the first complete (36-volume) edition of his work.
1897	'On the Idea of Comedy and the Uses of the Comic Spirit' published by Constable as *Essay on Comedy and the Uses of the Comic Spirit.*
1898	*Odes in Contribution to the Song of French History* appear in *Cosmopolis* in March. Daughter-in-law Daisy's edition of T*he George Meredith Birthday Book* published by Constable.
1901	*A Reading of Life, with Other Poems* published by Constable.
1905	Receives the Order of Merit.
1909	Catches chill; dies 18 May.

Abbreviations and References

References to *The Egoist* and 'An Essay on Comedy' are to the Norton Critical Edition. All other references to Meredith's novels are to the Memorial Edition published by Constable (27 vols, 1909–11). The novels in Constable's Standard Edition (17 vols, 1914–20) lack illustrations but have the same pagination as those in its Memorial Edition. Scribner's Memorial Edition published in New York (27 vols, 1909–12) was reset and is almost but not quite identical to the English one. References within the text to Meredith's novels consist of abbreviated title (see below), chapter number or heading (so that other editions may be consulted as well) and page numbers. Poems are cited by title and (if so divided) part. Parts are given in roman numbers. The text used here was Phyllis Bartlett's *The Poems of George Meredith* (2 vols, 1978). See Bibliography for fuller details of these and the parenthetically cited works listed below.

AHR	*The Adventures of Harry Richmond*
AM	*The Amazing Marriage*
BC	*Beauchamp's Career*
CH	*Meredith: The Critical Heritage*, ed. Ioan Williams
Chloe	'The Tale of Chloe'
CS	*Celt and Saxon*
DC	*Diana of the Crosssways*
E	*The Egoist*
EC	'An Essay on Comedy'
EH	*Evan Harrington*
F	*Farina*
Letters	*Letters*, ed. C. L. Cline (3 vols)
LO	*Lord Ormont and His Aminta*
MO	'Modern Love'
Norton	The Norton Critical Edition of *The Egoist* with 'An Essay on Comedy'
OC	*One of Our Conquerors*

ABBREVIATIONS AND REFERENCES

ORF	*The Ordeal of Richard Feverel*
RF	*Rhoda Fleming*
SB	*Sandra Belloni*
SL	*Selected Letters*, ed. Mohammad Shaheen
SS	*The Shaving of Shagpat*
V	*Vittoria*

Introduction

George Meredith came to be seen as the last of the Victorian sages, something that did his reputation more harm than good in the long run.[1] Yet his stance was anything but sage-like. He was an ebullient figure, hugely inventive and brimming with humour: 'chaff you he would', remembered one young family friend, 'in prose, in verse, in parables, in grotesque images, the whole wafted along by gales of laughter'.[2] Far from being moral diatribes, his works were intended to stimulate and provoke. They still do both. Largely through the operation of the comic principle, they challenge us to take the measure of ourselves, and find our true place in an ever-changing universe.

The best known of these works are his probing and innovative sonnet sequence 'Modern Love', and his virtuoso comic novel, *The Egoist*, along with the *Essay on Comedy* that preceded it. Also still admired and studied are his early Bildungsromans, *The Ordeal of Richard Feverel* and *The Adventures of Harry Richmond*; his political novel, *Beauchamp's Career*; and *Diana of the Crossways*, inspired by the real-life struggles of Lady Caroline Norton to cope with the consequences of a failed marriage. Readers of these works are drawn into an unusual dialogue with the author – surely one of the age's most intriguing personalities – and repaid with a keen sense of lived experience. This not only sheds light on the Victorian period, but regularly surprises us into making fresh and, it seems, personal discoveries about human nature. Such moments of surprise are among the greatest rewards of reading Meredith.

The novels, with their unconventional plots and unforgettable characters, can be riveting. In the best-known episode in *The Adventures of Harry Richmond*, the young hero realizes that the mounted figure in the equestrian monument at Sarkeld in the

Austrian Alps is actually his father. At the first flicker of life in the 'statue', the spectators gathered for the unveiling ceremony fall back 'with amazed exclamations'. The hitherto unsuspecting reader is similarly checked. When the apparently bronze figure moves, speaks, and dismounts to embrace him, Harry is frozen: 'I was unable to give out a breath', he confesses (*AHR* 16; 197). The reader too is momentarily stunned. It is some time before Harry's feelings thaw and he can be at ease with his father again. Then he must part from him and hurry on towards the next stage of his picaresque travels and independent life, sweeping the reader along in his wake. Meredith's vitality is contagious, invigorating. He makes us feel, like Harry and his friend Temple, that adventures (including the adventure of reading) are 'the only things worth living for' (*AHR* 20; 226).

As dynamic in mind as in personality, Meredith was fully engaged in the intellectual ferment of his age. *Beauchamp's Career* is shot through with his experience of helping his friend Admiral Maxse canvas for votes in Southampton. As for the eponymous Diana, she astounds Sir Lukin early on in her story by talking about the Repeal of the Corn Laws, because she is so different from his dreadful image of a radical woman. She is just one of the feisty heroines through whom Meredith projects his views on the 'Woman Question'. Such heroines are 'new women' before the 'New Woman' really arrives at the end of the century.[3] Elsewhere, it is evolution that most concerns him. Meredith was recognized long ago as an 'evolutionary philosopher',[4] and, along with his feminism (to which it is related), this has become a particularly fruitful area for recent scholarly research. The focus here has been on the poetry, and also on *The Egoist*, where Sir Willoughby Patterne believes that science has become 'the sole object worth a devoted pursuit' (*E* 3; 21). Willoughby misunderstands, or rather misapplies, Darwinism; but Meredith himself has thoroughly understood and assimilated it. His concern with the 'flourishing of the spirit' above and beyond the self had blossomed during his formative schooldays in Germany (*Letters* II: 910), and he finds his own way of developing it in poems like 'In the Woods' and 'The Woods of Westermain'. Wary of more rigid systems of philosophy, such as Auguste Comte's Positivism to which friends like G. H. Lewes and Leslie Stephen were more drawn,[5] he also became increasingly suspicious of organized religion. In general, a sense of man's fundamentally unmediated connection to nature links everything in Meredith's thinking, and leavens and illuminates everything he wrote.

If Meredith distils and contributes to the debates of his age, he is also a forerunner of our own in the way he communicates them. In his early fantasies, he experiments with what would now be called magic realism, and in *Harry Richmond* he explores and evokes the evolving consciousness, throwing a unique light on early experience. Eschewing pat answers, he subverts the conventional form of the novel by engaging his characters in situations and dialogues where their feelings are thwarted, their identities undermined, their words divorced from their meanings. The resultant narratives, with their metafictional commentaries, their obliquities and omissions, are of a kind to which recent dialogic critical approaches provide useful keys; such approaches help us catch the misinterpretations of characters like Willoughby, or Victor Radnor, the self-centred hero of *One of Our Conquerors*, and sieve their responses for the truth. Meanwhile, working and reworking his themes in the context of his wide reading and current discourse, Meredith affords many examples of now-fashionable intertextuality. His particular understanding of women's emotions and frustrations, their relationships with each other as well as with men, deserves all the praise it has been given.

Even Meredith's style, despite being as quirky, self-conscious and over-embellished as High Victorian architecture, has acquired a contemporary feel. Its figurative extravagance seems partly to have come naturally to him, and partly to have emanated from what Virginia Woolf calls his 'defiance of the ordinary' (Norton 533). But it has other, more specific purposes. Seymour Austin in *Beauchamp's Career* points out that metaphors permit 'condensation, as the hieroglyphists put an animal for a paragraph' (*BC* 28; 300). They can also serve to protect against the rawness of experience, as the narrator explains in *Diana of the Crossways*, where they help the heroine to confront her problems indirectly, to 'distinguish the struggle she was undergoing' (*DC* 24; 275). Most significantly, throughout Meredith's work, related images work beneath the surface of the text to weave deeper layers of meaning. What is packed can be unpacked, a challenge to which twenty-first century readers are well equipped to rise.

Amid welcome signs of renewed critical interest, this study seeks to place Meredith's better-known poetry and prose in the context of his life and work as a whole, and to reveal a fascinating, innovative author whose overriding concern with man's place in the natural scheme of things is more relevant than ever to us today.

1

A Life in Stages

YOUTH

Meredith's comparatively lowly origins both drove him to invention, and afforded him material for his novels. Born on 12 February 1828, he was the first and only child of a tailor and naval outfitter, Augustus Meredith, and his wife Jane, née Macnamara. He would offer different accounts of his place of birth, but it was probably the family home on Portsmouth High Street. His parents' surnames suggest that he was of Welsh and Irish stock, which gave him something else to play with later. He would always have a soft spot for the Celt – for example, he evokes a lyrically Welsh background for the beautiful, self-sacrificing heroine of 'The Tale of Chloe' (Chloe 9; 254). But both sides of his own family had been in Hampshire for generations. Augustus had inherited the business from his locally-born father Melchizidec, an almost legendary figure who later loomed large in Meredith's imaginative life. The chief outfitter to a dashing clientele, Melchizidec, like his namesake 'The Great Mel' in *Evan Harrington*, had considered himself a gentleman and lived accordingly.[1] When he died at 51 he passed on his debts to his wife Anne and only surviving son. Then on track for a career in medicine, Augustus was hopelessly ill-suited to rescuing the family's finances, even with his mother's help. Shortly after his marriage to Jane and the birth of their son George, 'Mrs Mel', who was ten years her husband's senior, died too, and the business slid inexorably towards bankruptcy.

Worse was to come. Jane herself died when the boy was 5. Soon after being declared bankrupt, Augustus set off to try to improve his fortunes in London, once there marrying the young woman who had come to keep house for him in the Portsmouth establishment. 'Housekeeper; yes, I remember hearing housekeeper. I think so. Housekeeper? yes, oh yes', says Lord Palmet, reporting a remark that would have far-reaching consequences in *Beauchamp's Career* (*BC* 31; 351). Young 'Gentleman Georgy'[2], who already liked to cut a bit of a dash, was withdrawn from his first school, St Paul's in Southsea, and left to the care of relatives with a farm in the Petersfield area. From here he was probably shunted off to a boarding-school outside Hampshire, in Lowestoft. Supporting evidence comes from a comment by Meredith himself, [3] and from the end of Chapter 4 of *Harry Richmond*, which describes a fairly long carriage-trip to such an establishment, where the new pupil's longing for his lost father is poignantly evoked.

Not that Augustus had stepped out of his son's life completely. His first wife had left their child a small legacy, augmented later by money from her sister's estate. In August 1841, Augustus duly applied to Chancery on the boy's behalf for extra funds to be released for his education and upkeep.[4] A year later, while still a ward in Chancery, Meredith was dispatched to the Moravian Brothers School at Neuwied in the Rhineland. This was an enlightened choice. Run along the liberal lines established by Comenius in Prerau, Austria, in the early seventeenth century, the school aimed to educate the whole child in a Christian ethos. Neuwied was a popular destination for children from progressive families at this time, giving opportunities for cultural interchange, language learning, and especially, as the young schoolteacher Matthew Weyburn puts it in Meredith's *Lord Ormont and His Aminta*, for the 'practical Englishman to settle his muzzle in a nosebag of ideas'. It was Meredith's most formative experience, and he returned from it around a year and a half later[5] just as Weyburn envisaged his own pupils returning, 'with the whoop of the mountains in [him] and ready to jump out' (*LO* 24; 287).

The religious atmosphere of the school had also made an impact on him. Two of his farewell letters have only recently been published. One, in German, expressed his gratitude to Baron Jannasch, thought to have been director of the school. Sometimes, says Meredith, we forget God's rules, and therefore 'cannot control ourselves and insult our fellow men or hurt their feelings. As there are few, almost none, whom I have not hurt', he continues, 'I should like to apologise to you and all [everybody]' (trans. in *SL*, 18). In the other letter, written in English, he tells a young friend that it is hard to find someone whose 'temper disposition and actions agree with one's own' (*SL*, 18), and confesses to having 'found it impossible' to change these things in himself without God's help. Although he would continue to refer to God from time to time, the piety would soon be subsumed into a sense of spiritual connection with nature;[6] but Meredith's awareness of some jangling core of being, needing to be acknowledged and curbed, would persist. He would later label it egoism, and see the failure to admit to and overcome it as the main barrier to living a full life – and indeed to human progress. It became his chief bugbear, which he would expend much of his creative energy attacking, to both tragic and comic effect.

Augustus Meredith stepped into his son's life again after his return, making another application to Chancery for funds for an apprenticeship. The process was long drawn out, and in the interval Meredith probably returned to and helped at his relatives' farm. Here too support comes from the fiction: 'I stated that I liked farms', says the eponymous Harry Richmond stoutly, having enjoyed nothing better than supping along with the farm labourers at Dipwell (*AHR* 7; 94). Eventually, negotiations with a bookseller and small-scale publisher having fallen through, Meredith was articled to a lawyer, entering Richard Charnock's office in February 1846.

Legal training seems an unlikely choice for someone of Meredith's unconventional background and exuberance, but then Charnock was no typical lawyer. He published works not only on legal matters but also on etymology and anthropology, as well as travel guides – including one to the Tyrol – acquiring a doctorate from the University of Göttingen. Meredith appears to mock him in the character of Richard's uncle Hippias in *The Ordeal of Richard Feverel* in 1859, a man once seen as the bright spark of the family, but who fell prey to dyspepsia, and gave up his own prospects as a lawyer to compile a hefty tome on European fairy tales. Yet, at the time, Charnock had a huge influence on his new clerk. Taken up by the lawyer's coterie of literary and artistic friends, Meredith contributed his first published work to the handwritten journal they circulated, the *Monthly Observer*. One of his poems here, 'Chillianwallah', commemorating a recent bloodbath of a battle in the Anglo-Sikh Second War, was then printed in *Chambers's Journal* in July 1849. Possibly 'the worst he ever published',[7] the poem was nevertheless rhythmic and topical, and chimed with the widespread distress at the East India Company's failure to rout the Sikh army. Meredith also took his turn in editing the journal – a useful experience, since he would one day, albeit briefly, edit the *Fortnightly Review*.

Neuwied had given the young clerk a lifelong love of rambling. Escaping office work and his rented room in Pimlico, he would walk out through Chelsea into Middlesex and beyond. In another early poem, 'Invitation to the Country', he asks the city dweller to 'Cast off the yoke of toil and smoke' and immerse himself in the pleasures of spring, birdsong particularly. His usual companion on these rambles was another contributor to the *Monthly Observer*, Edward Peacock. A few years older than he was, Peacock was a clerk at the East India Office where his father, the satirist Thomas Love Peacock, was Chief Examiner – hence perhaps Meredith's keen interest in the debacle at Chillianwallah. The two young men had a special reason to strike out for the Middlesex/Surrey border. This was the

Peacock's Thames-side house on Lower Halliford Green
(photograph by the present author)

countryside Edward knew best, since his family home was at Lower Halliford in Shepperton, on the Middlesex bank of the Thames. Some time before August 1849, Meredith was taken there to be introduced to Peacock himself, not simply as his son's friend, but as a prospective son-in-law.

THE BIRTH OF LOVE

Inevitably, as Virginia Woolf put it, after 'Youth' had come 'The Birth of Love' (Norton, 534). Young, energetic, and emotionally naïve, impressionable himself and longing to impress others, Meredith had been ripe for romance. Edward had a widowed sister, Mary Ellen Nicolls, who often stayed with her brother in London, and who was also an *Observer* contributor. Nearly seven years older than Meredith (a gap he later exaggerated, as if to explain their incompatibility), she had known great tragedy: in 1844, her young husband, Lieutenant Edward Nicolls, had died in a rescue attempt which she herself had urged on him, when on board his ship in the Shannon estuary. She had been pregnant at the time, and now her little girl, Ellen, was being looked after in Lower Halliford by the women in the Peacock household – her sister Rosa, and Peacock's adopted daughter May – while she was in town. Still in her 20s, Mary Ellen was beautiful, clever and vivacious, and Meredith fell under her spell. She, for her part, admired his literary gifts. With hindsight, her friend Anne Bennett doubted that their relationship was really based on love,[8] but after repeated proposals Meredith finally won her hand.

Their marriage got off to a flying start with a wedding at St George's, Hanover Square, London. Peacock himself signed the register. Meredith had come into his legacy now, and the couple honeymooned in Europe. On their return, still riding high, they took lodgings at The Limes, rather a grand establishment just over the river from Shepperton in the fine old Surrey town of Weybridge. The Limes was run by Elizabeth Maceroni, widow of a dashing Italian colonel who had been nicknamed 'Count Maceroni'; the aristocratic novelist Edward Bulwer-Lytton, and the artist William Frith, are said to have stayed there.[9] Meredith's happiness during this period is reflected in *Poems* of 1851, his first independent publication. This self-financed volume sold badly and received generally poor reviews; it embarrassed him later. But it is full of enthusiasm for life, and inspirational in its belief in the enlargement of the soul through union with the natural universe. One particular poem, 'Love in the Valley', caught the public eye; to the fledgling poet's delight, Tennyson himself admired it. It was a propitious enough debut, then, and some readers, like William Sharp (a.k.a. the writer Fiona MacLeod), have wished 'that, in his later poetry, Meredith had oftener sounded the simple and beautiful pastoral note which gave so lovely a beauty to his first volume of verse'.[10]

While staying at The Limes, Meredith met the Duff Gordons, a titled couple then spending their summers at nearby Nutfield Cottage with Lady Duff Gordon's parents, the Austins. This gave him an entry into a new cultural milieu, introducing him to people like Tom Taylor, a future editor of *Punch*, who became both a useful contact and a lifelong friend. On one of his visits he was held spellbound by the tale of a serpent-queen related by another of the Duff Gordons' guests. He himself began spinning yarns about such a personage to 8-year-old Janet, the Duff Gordons' daughter, while carrying her home from play-dates with Edith Nicolls. Thus was born the tale of Bhanavar the Beautiful, as told by Shibli the barber in the second chapter of *The Shaving of Shagpat*. Published in 1854, this first full-length narrative did for Meredith's prose what *Poems* (1851) did for his poetry, introducing many of its later characteristics. Here already are his bitten-off phrases and accumulative conceits, his predilection for fantasy and the subversion of literary convention, his assertive heroines, and the sometimes comically flawed heroes who require their governance and have to take a buffeting from life before (if they are lucky) winning them. Little Janet was not the only one to be enchanted by these flights of imagination: George Eliot loved *Shagpat* too, astutely noting the author's 'genuine love and mental affinity' for this kind of story-telling (*CH*, 47). The *jeu d'ésprit* was the young Meredith's natural form.

But this golden period was already ending. His legacy had been a small one, and, with any thought of a legal career behind him, he was making next to nothing by the pen. Moreover, little as he cared for Victorian notions of respectability, Meredith still could not bear to be known as (in the lisping words of the eponymous Evan Harrington as a young boy) 'the thon of a thnip' (*EH* 44; 542). Not given to restraint, he tried posturing instead, putting it about that he was the descendant of Celtic chieftains. He came to see the folly of this, poking fun at Evan's father in the novel by saying that 'Nothing less than being born in St James's Square would content old Mel, and he must have a Marquis for his father' (22; 282). But it was a folly never quite conquered. He was always prone to obfuscate or glamorize his past, perhaps in order to blot out painful memories. He appears to have covered up his father's trade even from his new wife, with painful repercussions. The year he married, his father had emigrated to South Africa, where he now had a tailor's shop in Cape Town. Not long afterwards, Mary Ellen discovered a bill he sent his son, for forwarding to a customer.[11] She felt deceived; by the time of the 1851 census, Meredith was staying in more ordinary accommodation behind the High Street, while Mary Ellen and her little girl were in Shepperton again with her father. Their problems are echoed in a children's book published by Emilie Maceroni, one of Mrs Maceroni's talented daughters, at this time. Dedicated to Mrs Austin, Lady Duff Gordon's mother, *Magic Words* depicts a writer separated from his wife, and reunited with her at Christmas by a child's insistence on forgiveness.

The marriage limped on for several years, producing one son, Arthur, born at Peacock's house in 1853. Soon afterwards, the young family were together again, and moved (or were persuaded to move) into the rather cramped Vine Cottage on Russell Road, just across the green. At this time, Mary Ellen thought up a scheme to augment the family income by running a servant-girls' school. It came to nothing, but indicates the strain the marriage was under. Indeed, she now seems to have been having an affair with Charles Mansfield, a charismatic Weybridge-based scientist and polymath whom she had contacted about her proposed school, and who died in agony in 1855 from chemical burns received in his laboratory.[12] If the two had been in love, this would have been one of many romantic entanglements for him, and only the latest in several tragedies for her. Arthur had been preceded by miscarriages and stillbirths, and in 1851 Mary Ellen had also lost her mother, who had never got over losing a child of her own. A highly-strung, passionate woman herself, Mary Ellen found the various stresses of these years unendurable. Catherine Horne, wife of the Victorian editor and adventurer Richard (later Hengist) Horne, who had helped Meredith publish 'Chillianwallah', spent three weeks with the Merediths in the late autumn of 1852. She sent her husband a startling account of a quarrel, during which Mary Ellen screamed loudly and seemed suicidal, only to dress for Sunday dinner with her father afterwards as if nothing had happened. 'What a strange nature he must have to bear this, and still retain his affection for her', she wrote, adding, 'How will it end?' (*SL*, 28).

The marriage finally collapsed completely in 1857, when Mary Ellen went off to Wales with the young painter Henry Wallis. It was a humiliating double blow for Meredith, because Wallis was a

The beleaguered writer and his young sympathizer, as illustrated by E. H. Wehnert in *The Magic Words: A Tale for Christmas Time* (Cundell & Addey, 1851), following p.10

friend, for whose acclaimed painting of Thomas Chatterton he had recently modelled. Perhaps Mary Ellen turned to Wallis more for solace than love; perhaps neither expected the relationship to last.[13] But a letter she sent him that year suggests otherwise: 'I am always dreading to lose you because I feel I have no right to you', she wrote, 'and I love you so really, so far beyond anything I have known of love' (SL, 31). She looks soulfully at the artist in his pencil portrait of her in 1858.

Undeterred by the mainly tepid reception of his second romantic fantasy, *Farina: A Legend of Cologne*, Meredith had started a realistic novel, *The Ordeal of Richard Feverel*, while Mary Ellen was pregnant with Wallis's child. Richard first glimpses the heroine Lucy while boating on a stretch of river with a rushing weir, in a setting very like that of Shepperton where the author's own romance had blossomed. To have lost this 'Eden' became a crucial part of the life-experience with which Meredith worked in his novels. With this for his material, too, his sonnet cycle of 1862, 'Modern Love', focused not on union but on alienation. Far from offering fulfilment and lasting happiness, marriage, it seemed, could be nothing but a battleground, a 'wedded lie' (ML XXXV). This discovery was all the more devastating because it threatened his whole vision of life; but, in the event, Meredith was not crushed by the experience, rescuing something positive from it even within the work itself. Having written it off in 'little more than three months',[14] he was then able to put these traumatic events behind him in his poetry, and examine them more objectively in his fiction.

RECOVERY

Luckily, Meredith's temperament differed from that of Chatterton, who had taken arsenic under the twin pressures of rejection and poverty. Far from desponding after Mary Ellen left him, or perhaps in the battle against despondency, he became more active than ever. He moved from a temporary address in West Brompton back to Surrey, where he and Arthur lodged first at the top of Esher High Street with one of the Queen's favourite sculptors, Francis John Williamson, and then some distance behind the High Street at the quieter Copsham Cottage, where he remained until the summer of 1864. But he was not isolated. He had a great talent for friendship, and his friends came from the top echelons of all walks of life. A particular favourite was Captain Frederick Maxse, whom he had met in 1858, and whose character and radicalism inspired the hero of *Beauchamp's Career*. Another close friend was the barrister and editor William Hardman, a hearty, rotund man whom Meredith addressed as Tuck, beloved Tuck, Lord Tuck and so forth in their correspondence, signing himself off as Robin. Hardman also took a house in Esher for the summer of 1861, and accompanied him on many of his subsequent rambles, sometimes for miles across county to Haslemere on the Surrey border. Hardman would feature as the reliable and (despite his politics) likable Tory lawyer Blackburn Tuckham in *Beauchamp's Career*.

During these Esher years, Meredith's London circle widened too. He had made the acquaintance of the artist John Everett Millais in his Weybridge days. Another founding member of the Pre-Raphaelite Brotherhood, William Rossetti, had reviewed *Poems: 1851* favourably in the *Critic*. In about 1861, Meredith got to know William's brother Dante Gabriel as well. When a damning review of 'Modern Love' appeared in the *Spectator* of 24 May 1862, the poet Algernon Swinburne, who was closely associated with the Brotherhood, took up cudgels on his behalf, writing a letter of protest to the magazine and praising Meredith as 'one of the leaders of English literature' (*CH*, 97). Since becoming literary adviser and reader for the publishers Chapman & Hall in August 1860, Meredith had needed to spend some nights in London, and in the summer of 1862 his friendship with this group was sealed when he agreed to become a sub-tenant along with both Swinburne and William Rossetti of Dante Gabriel's recently leased house, 'a strange, quaint, grand old place' at 16 Cheyne Walk, in Chelsea (*Letters* I: 149). But the companionship of these excitable, temperamental artists proved even less conducive to work than lodging with a sculptor, and he soon withdrew from the arrangement.

Meredith fell in love again twice during the early 1860s. First came his brief romance with Janet Duff Gordon, no longer a child, but only 17. He was still legally married then, and in charge of young Arthur – whom Janet tutored in German and cared for while Meredith was in London. She ended up marrying someone even older than 'her Poet', the banker and hobby-archaeologist Henry Ross, accompanying him to Alexandria. But, like Mary Ellen, she left her mark on Meredith's work. In the least deviously autobiographical of his novels, *Evan Harrington* (subtitled, significantly enough, 'He Would Be a Gentleman'), the Great Mel's son aspires for the hand of Rose Jocelyn, a girl far above him in social class. '*Evan Harrington* was *my* novel, because Rose Jocelyn was myself',[15] claimed Janet later, with considerable justification. Meredith wrote to her affectionately on her engagement to Ross. Their friendship not only survived but lasted a lifetime.

Millais' illustration for 'The Meeting', a short lyric published in *Once a Week* in September 1862. A girl who has been 'ruined' hugs her infant close as she passes a young man on the heath. The man has his own 'lawless love', but the two exchange wistful looks – a poignant moment perfectly captured by the artist. Reprinted in the Memorial Edition of the poems, Vol. 24, following p.146.

In October 1861 one obstacle to Meredith's remarrying was removed. Mary Ellen died in nearby Oatlands, never having recovered either strength or spirits after the birth of her son by Wallis. Although Wallis had left her by then, Meredith neither visited her in her last illness, nor attended her funeral at St Nicholas Church, Shepperton. He was better able to work out his bitterness in his creative work than in the real world. But soon after her death, he told Maxse that he began to feel 'new life', and to wonder, when responding to the invitation to Maxse's wedding, 'whether any nice woman will ever look on me' (*Letters* I: 121). First, however, he went travelling on the Continent in the summers of 1861 and 1863, and, like so many English writers, became enamoured of Italy. This was when he repaid Emilie Macaroni's compliment with compound interest, making her the heroine of his two Italian novels, *Emilia in England* (later published as *Sandra Belloni*), and its sequel *Vittoria*, in which she blossoms into 'an animated picture of ideal Italia', a *cantatrice* capable of stirring her audience to a 'tremendous frenzy' (*V* 20; 222, 224). However, the woman Meredith finally proposed to in the spring of 1864 was of a different type, a calm, affectionate young person of Huguenot extraction then living in Mickleham with her widowed French father, a retired wool-merchant. Frederick Sandys's portrait of Marie Vulliamy suggests that though tall and already rather matronly she was a gentle soul, and Meredith confirms this in a letter to the Rev. Augustus Jessopp, headmaster at the King Edward VI School in Norwich where he had now sent Arthur. 'Some vitality being wanted', he admits, 'but the lack of it partially compensated by so very much sweetness' (*Letters* I: 255). Volatile women, it seems, were best kept inside the covers of books. When Meredith had at last passed muster with Marie's father,[16] the couple were married by Jessopp at St Michael and All Angels, Mickleham, in September 1864. Janet Ross attended the ceremony with her father, Sir Alexander Duff Gordon, the inspiration for Rose's father Sir Frank Jocelyn in *Evan Harrington*.

MATURITY

Rather like one of his own heroes, Meredith had advanced to

maturity in a series of dramatic episodes; now he could settle down. After another spell in lodgings in Esher, the couple took a three-year lease on a house called Kingston Lodge in nearby Norbiton, where they had their first child, William Maxse, named in honour of both William Hardman and Frederick Maxse. But they left at the end of 1867 to move into Flint Cottage early in the following year, 'a small cottage in very beautiful country', as he accurately described it (*SL*, 72), just above Burford Bridge on the lower slopes of Box Hill. There in July 1871 they had another child, a little girl called Marie Eveleen, soon to be known as Mariette or Riette: 'I walked to the doctor at Dorking and again – you should have seen me! – I drove his white horse for obstetric instruments' he wrote to Hardman, saying that the birth had been 'a Titanic struggle' (*SL*, 58). The man who had told Marie's sister Katherine in June 1864, a few months before his Mickleham wedding, that he had 'never had sister, or brother, or family, or love' (*SL*, 41), had finally got a stable home life.

Neither of his mid-1860s' novels – *Vittoria*, set largely in Milan during the Italian uprising of 1848, and *Rhoda Fleming*, with its focus on fallen women and class issues – had fared well. But at Box Hill the tide turned, as he had prophesied it would when he first fell in love with Marie: 'I shall work as I have never yet done'.[17] Living up to Swinburne's claim for him, he established himself solidly at last in the world of letters. From R. H. Hutton in the *Spectator*, who had been so hard on him before, came an acknowledgement of 'originality, wealth of conception, genius' in *The Adventures of Harry Richmond* (*CH*, 159), while *Beauchamp's Career* also won good reviews in some prominent journals, notably the *Pall Mall Gazette*. Meredith's theories in *An Essay on Comedy*, first given as a talk at the London Institute in 1877, also had their effect – especially when embodied in *The Egoist*, his witty and perceptive novel of 1879. Here, a heroine with some of the spirit of Meredith's first wife humiliates a posturing tyrant who, as Meredith himself admitted, has a great deal of his author in him. The tragedy of his early manhood has been completely reworked and served up by the mature Meredith as an entertainment; in this new form, it sparkles.

By now, the Merediths had had a two-room writing chalet built at the top of their sloping garden. Filling it with tobacco smoke, he could write uninterruptedly there, talking freely to his characters. To John Morley, then editor of the *Fortnightly Review*, he wrote on 5 April 1877, soon after its completion,

> I work and sleep up in my cottage at present, and anything grander than the days and nights at my porch you will not find away from the Alps; for the dark line of my hill runs up to the stars, the valley below is a soundless gulf. There I pace like a shipman before turning in. In the day, with the south-west blowing, I have a brilliant universe rolling up to me. (*Letters* I: 539)

That he shut himself off there like a hermit might seem ironic, considering how he had longed for domestic relationships. But few men of his time expected to cut much of a figure in the house, and the arrangement suited him.

Popular success followed critical approval with the publication in 1885 of *Diana of the Crossways*. Readers knew what to expect from him now, and were less fazed by his idiosyncratic style and abrupt shifts of scene and tone. Moreover, literary taste had to some degree caught up with him. As reader for Chapman & Hall, Meredith had committed an error of commercial judgement by turning down Mrs Wood's *East Lynne* early in the 1860s. But sentimentalism of Mrs Wood's kind was

Meredith's writing chalet in the heart of nature, on the lower slopes of Box Hill (photograph by the present author)

waning at last, and, thanks to Darwin, naturalism (focusing on the evolution of character in response to inborn traits and life experiences) was in the ascendancy. By now, too, and not unconnected with this, the social problem novel had become a genre of its own, with the Woman Question prominent amongst its concerns. *Diana*, with its emotional complexity and candour, and its echoes of a real-life, high-profile struggle, was perfect for its time. It went to three editions in as many months.

AGE

Meredith's career now enters its final stage. He never repeated this popular success, but during his later years at Box Hill his stock rose higher and higher. Although even more stylistically challenging than usual, *One of Our Conquerors* appeared not only in the *Fortnightly*, but also in the *Australasian* and *The New York Sun*. The shorter, more accessible *Lord Ormont and His Aminta* appeared a couple of years later in the *Pall Mall Gazette*, and his last complete novel, *The Amazing Marriage*, in *Scribner's*. All three works pushed hard against Victorian morality and mores, especially as they impinged on women. Meanwhile, *Richard Feverel*, which had seemed so revolutionary at first, now became 'a cultural icon'.[18] One of Meredith's most appreciative readers was Oscar Wilde, who in his 1891 dialogue-essay 'The Critic as Artist' famously described Meredith as a 'prose Browning', something that must have pleased Meredith, once a member of the Browning Society (see *SL*, 78). Wilde's approval itself seems appropriate: both authors were masters of discomfiture and witty dialogue. In these years too Meredith wrote a good deal of new poetry, and saw his work come out in uniform editions. Replacing Tennyson as President of the Society of Authors in 1892, and receiving the Order of Merit for his services to literature in 1905, were both marks of his now widespread recognition. He had become the Grand Old Man of English letters. Flora Thompson's Laura makes a pilgrimage to Box Hill, content just to look at Flint Cottage from the outside;[19] authors as diverse as James Barrie and Sir Arthur Conan Doyle beat a path to his door, as did Robert Louis Stevenson, Henry James and Thomas Hardy, to whom he had once given advice as a publisher's reader. A letter of appreciation presented to him on his 70th birthday was signed by these stars in the literary firmament, and many more.

However, the last two decades of Meredith's life really did amount to the 'long last sigh' described in his poem, 'Youth and Age'. In 1886, the year following his success with *Diana*, he had lost his supportive wife, Marie, to throat cancer. Only a few years later, his son Arthur died of consumption, having been nursed at the end by Mary Ellen's first child, his half-sister Edith. Hardman had died just a week after Arthur, and Maxse in 1900. Despite Meredith's own apparent robustness, he had long been subject to stomach problems, and had taxed his frame by his pastime of hurling around a weight that he nicknamed 'the beetle'; in 1905, suffering from the paralyzing effects of a spinal disorder, the once tireless rambler, who had walked the length and breadth of the county with Leslie Stephen and his fellow 'Sunday Tramps', found it difficult even to get to his writing chalet, confessing to Lady Ottoline Morrell that he now smoked in the main house, making Flint Cottage a 'tobacco-box' (*SL*, 184). He would still send friends to look at the ancient twisted yews in Druid's Grove in nearby Norbury Park, his inspiration for 'The Woods of Westermain', but was only able to view such places himself from a bath chair pulled by his donkey, Picnic. Longer trips were taken by car. He also became practically stone-deaf.

Meredith died in May 1909, and, because of his religious unorthodoxy and by his own wish, his ashes were interred in the local cemetery at Dorking beside his wife instead of in Westminster Abbey. Although a late and as-yet unpublished letter suggests that his reputation had already started to decline,[20] the king himself sent condolences to the bereaved family: 'His Majesty, together with the country, sincerely laments the loss of so great a novelist and writer',[21] and the great and the good attended the funeral, among them Hardy, Kipling, Conan Doyle, Henry James, Rider Haggard, James Barrie, the Holman-Hunts, Philip Burne-Jones (Edward Burne-Jones's son), and Mary Watts (the artist G. F. Watts's widow), and so on. The Welsh Folksong Society was represented there too, which would doubtless have pleased him greatly. Barrie recorded the event, and whimsically imagined Meredith striding energetically uphill to join the immortals after the hearse had passed by with its little casket of his ashes.[22] But the epitaph on the book-shaped headstone, taken from *Vittoria*, struck an earnestly Victorian note:

> 'Our life is but a little holding, lent
> To do a mighty labour: we are one
> With heaven and the stars when it is spent
> To serve God's name: else die we with the sun.'
>
> (*V* 21; 252)

Lacking birth and breeding, and for a long time love, Meredith had indeed done his 'mighty labour', rising above his insecurities to produce some of the most distinctive works of his age – or of any other. The reputation he gained in later years would slump dramatically as he faded from living memory. But, paradoxically, it continued for the best part of a century to obscure the real nature of his achievement as a writer.

2

Poems (1851) and 'Modern Love'

NATURE IN *POEMS* (1851)

Meredith was a poet first and last: 'I began with poetry and I shall finish with it', he told his friend Edward Clodd in later life.[1] Eager to impress with his debut volume, the young man dedicated it to Peacock, and quoted from Horne's popular epic *Orion* on its title page. Then he presented copies to various other men of letters. With a mixture of pride and humility, he told A. J. Scott, Professor of English at University College, London, that he wished the poems 'to be considered more as *indications* than accomplishments'. Later, however, he dismissed the whole thing as his 'boy's book' (*Letters* I: 18, 110), destroying his unbound copies of it. Critics have generally accepted the later verdict, but William Sharp was not alone in appreciating its freshness, while Mark Pattison recognized early on that his mature poetry developed 'germs' from it (*CH*, 249).

What it reveals most clearly is his focus on nature, not just as his inspiration or even as his spiritual guide. He finds its forces made manifest in his own being. His feelings as a young man in love are both derived from it, and directed towards it, so that union with it is partly a given, and partly a longed-for goal. In 'Song' ('Love within the lover's breast'), for example, the human emotion is expressed in a run of simple comparisons with nature:

> Love! thy love pours down on mine
> As the sunlight on the vine,
> As the snow-rill on the vale,
> As the salt breeze in the sail;

The analogies pile up, as they do in his prose, forcing him into some awkward accommodations: in the following lines he expresses his own response, saying, 'As the song unto the bird, / On my lips thy name is heard', with 'unto' apparently serving as 'of', to suit the metre. But another effect is to suggest that love, when given and returned, is elemental and dynamic, a natural phenomenon like the others that animate our universe. In 'Twilight Music', the bigger picture, in this case the natural harmony of spheres, stars and landscape, comes first. Then the whispering 'spiritual music' of the twilight and the 'sweet voice' of the loved one are mingled, and the speaker responds. In this way the music is gradually married with 'the human lyre, / Blending divine delight with loveliest desire'. Despite some derivative collocations, and a drift away from the tightly rhymed form of the first half, this poem is more than a youthful exercise. The evocation of cosmic energy in the twilight, the way it inspires both the natural scene and the lover's own ardour, and above all the subtle way that the reader is drawn into the experience, make it already unmistakably Meredithian.

Even when the mood is reminiscent rather than ardent, man's receptiveness to natural beauty, and the potential for a kind of spiritual consummation through this, are keenly felt. Playing nostalgically over memories of the Rhineland, which he had revisited during his honeymoon with Mary Ellen, Meredith describes its

> distant village-roofs of blue and white,
> With intersections of quaint-fashioned beams
> All slanting crosswise, and the feudal gleams
> Of ruined turrets, barren in the light;

The human element, both past (the 'ruined turrets') and present (the 'village-roofs'), is integral to the rural scene; the watchers themselves, 'Sunspread, and shaded with a branching screen' ('Pictures of the Rhine: II'), derive pleasure from being a part of it too, as well from their own intimacy: 'Was ever such a happy morn as this! / Birds sing, we shout, flowers breathe, trees shine with one delight!' ('Pictures of the Rhine: III'). The long final lines here seem to be an early experiment in creating a distinctive sequence. There is passion in these 'Pictures', and vision, and a real sense of a young poet seeking his own way of involving the reader with them.

Although the Rhineland still tugs at his heart, Meredith is already finding his philosophical ideas best embodied in the 'charms of English home', in the various species of trees and birds, and the topography of the Surrey countryside with its heaths, hills, valleys and rivers:

There, by the wet-mirrored osiers, the emerald wing of the kingfisher
Flashes, the fish in his beak! there the dab-chick dived, and the motion
Lazily undulates all thro' the tall standing army of rushes.

('Pastorals: VII')

In this scene, all is movement, fast or slow; nothing is still. The sharp sense in such lines of the particular, lived experience comes from their having been inspired by specific locations: for example, Meredith could and (significantly) did tell Hardman the exact spot where he 'composed and wrote' the fifth of the seven 'Pastorals' printed in this first volume: 'it was on an eminence surrounded by pines on the St George's Hill estate' near where he and Mary Ellen were staying in Weybridge.[2] Again, in 'South-West Wind in the Woodland', he compares the 'music' of familiar, individual species of trees to other sounds, both natural and man-made:

> not trembling now
> The aspens, but like freshening waves
> That fall upon a shingly beach; –
> And round the oak a solemn roll
> Of organ harmony ascends,

Meredith describes this natural orchestration not just for its own sake, but to suggest that the individual who 'yields' to nature's voice and 'seats his soul upon her wings' will find a consummation in it, and never lose the knowledge and delight thus gained: 'For every elemental power / Is kindred to our hearts'; and 'Once taken to the unfettered sense, / Once claspt into the naked life, / The union is eternal'. In short, the euphoria inspired by the immediate experience would leave its mark forever on the person who experiences it.

Nothing tells more about Meredith than his fondness for the wind in the trees. One of his very earliest efforts had been a long, unfinished Wordsworthian narrative entitled 'Wandering Willie', in which he had written of the 'victory which, not in vain – / Is promised by the trumpet gale' (Canto 2). He would pick up the idea again and again, notably in his sonorous 'Ode to the Spirit of Earth in Autumn', which draws on parts of that early poem, and the brief but memorable 'Dirge in Woods'. In the latter, written on Marie's father's death, he says that 'we drop like the fruits of the tree' as 'the wind sways the pines' and the clouds race overhead. Meredith's philosophizing appeals most when embodied in this way, in his direct response to nature's energies. We find it in the novels, too, for instance in the great drenching storms of Chapter 42 of *Richard Feverel* and Chapter 26 of *The Egoist*. Entering his 60s, he would still say, 'The wind that blows is the wind that's best' ('A Stave of Roving Time'). It answered his own zest for movement, his need to feel exhilarated and swept up in the current of life, and his wish to sweep his readers up into it too.

For these early poems are by no means spontaneous effusions. Throughout, he adopts strict metrical arrangements and (often) rhyme schemes, as if needing to control the outpourings of a large, all-inclusive passion for life that might otherwise overwhelm him. He already has his audience in his sights, too, justifying the use of the 'blank octo-syllabic' verse form in 'South-West Wind in the Woodland', for instance, by saying that he wants to convey 'the reckless rushing rapidity, and sweeping sound of the great wind among the foliage . . . in such a manner that the ear should only be conscious of swiftness, and no sweetness'.[3] The aim from the start, then, is for readers to participate in his experience, and be borne along too, feeling themselves taken 'unfettered', as he puts it in that poem, into nature's embrace.

A sense of the precarious balance between form and feeling makes the best-known work here, 'Love in the Valley', especially effective. Apparently referring to an early romance with a younger, virginal woman, its regularly lilting cadences seem barely to contain the urgent desires, hesitations and worries of the equally inexperienced lover: 'What can have taught her distrust of all I tell her?', he wonders; or, 'Comes a sudden question – should a strange hand pluck her!' Again, however, he is buoyed up by his faith in the natural process. The girl herself is so closely identified with nature that she becomes '[f]ull of all the wildness of the woodland creatures', and there is much to suggest that, when the time is ripe, the mother who currently tends her and guards her from men's attentions will allow her to move on from youth through the natural sequence of mating and mothering. This is a fulfilment of the life cycle in which the lover joyfully anticipates playing his part: 'Lo! the nest is ready, let me not languish longer! / Bring her to my arms on the first May night'. The final stressed monosyllables sound confident as well as insistent. As usual, they make their impact on us. No wonder Tennyson went round the house 'chanting its cadences'.[4]

When not driven by his instincts and passion, Meredith asserted his claim to serious consideration by evoking his literary heritage – extolling the great poets of the past in a series of brief dactylic verses, and producing longer poems on overtly classical themes.[5] The former employ imitation as a form of homage, but the latter gave him the opportunity to write beyond his own experience. They also foreshadow some of the problems his readers would have with his later writings. In 'The Shipwreck of Idomeneus', for example, Idomeneus pledges what turns out to be the sacrifice of his own son to Poseidon, in return for his men's safe return to Crete. It is movingly done, the more so because Idomeneus feels intimations of his grief while the men are still sleeping off the storm. But the poem shows too the influence of James Macpherson, whose Ossianic epics were particularly popular on the Continent: 'The more imaginative and sensitive are sure to like him best', Meredith told Arthur later (*Letters* I: 459). The result here is an overload of epic similes, with, for example, the surging waves seen not just as the seahorses which are part of the Poseidon myth, but as thoroughbred mares with streaming manes, rearing and frothing at the bit, and so forth. Meredith would never lose his penchant for long figurative flurries, and gets caught up in extended metaphors even at dramatic moments in the novels.[6] The long ballad 'Daphne' shows a different kind of self-indulgence. Here, Meredith fleshes out the familiar myth with sensuous imagery, allowing Apollo to come to the very edge of the 'bridal bower' with Daphne before she is stricken with shame by Diana and takes flight. His 'sensuous warmth of image and expression' were noted in the first unsigned *Spectator* review of 22 August 1851, as something 'which, though not passing propriety, might as well be tempered' (*CH*, 29).

More intriguing in 'Daphne' is the miserable ending. At first, bindweed, woodbine and other trailing plants impede the once '[l]ove-suffused' Daphne's flight, but then she is saved from Apollo's advances by being subsumed into the vegetation. Apollo is shocked to encounter not her flesh but a mass of 'palpitating branches'; and, as Daphne is transformed into a laurel, her own last sentient impulses are not just of relief at her escape, but of sympathy for the god. Meredith deals elsewhere in this volume with the more ordinary human experience of change. In the much shorter lyric, 'Song' ('No, no, the falling blossom is no sign'), he acknowledges that love 'moves with life along a darker way', but characteristically allows us to come to terms with it by suggesting that even when 'young enchantment and romance' fade, the experience somehow lingers on in a general enrichment of lovers' lives.[7] In 'Daphne', however, all that is left of a passionate encounter is an echo 'travelling in the distance drear'. When Meredith sent Horne a poem about 'Daphne', he suggested it was a typical expression of how 'First love still follows the fair, fleeting shape!' (*Letters* I: 7). Unfortunately, this too was a hint of what was to come next, both in his own life and in his poetry.

HUMAN NATURE IN 'MODERN LOVE'

Meredith's concern with nature carried over into *Modern Love and Poems of the English Roadside, with Poems and Ballads* (1862), most obviously in poems like 'Ode to the Spirit of Earth in Autumn', with its celebration of the vibrant colours and stormy energy of the season, and its sudden, dramatic glimpse of a 'crimson-footed nymph' starting a satyr from the glade. Indeed, Meredith now tries to broaden his vision of nature to include not only the passionate, impulsive lover but all human society: the new volume has been described as 'a supremely political collection'.[8] In the Browningesque monologue entitled 'The Old Chartist', for example, the unrepentant campaigner sees 'a day when every pot will boil / Harmonious in one great Tea-garden!' But other poems give less ground for optimism. 'Juggling Jerry' is about an itinerant performer who is dying in his wife's arms. With his last breaths he challenges those who would sneer at his honest life's work: 'Haven't you juggled a vast amount?' he asks (V), implying a different and culpable sleight of hand in the world of affairs. As for 'Grandfather Bridgeman', the old man's boasts about his heroic soldier-grandson in the Crimea all turn to ashes when he sees the youth '[w]heeled, pale, in a chair, and shattered' after having been wounded at the Battle of Inkerman (XXXII). There is more here about human deception and self-deception than brotherhood or harmony. The predominant feeling is summed up in a brief lyric entitled 'I Chafe at Darkness', where the speaker feels his wings have been clipped, and laments, 'I have lost what made / The dawn-breeze magic'. The change is fully established in the fifty extended, sixteen-line sonnets that constitute 'Modern Love'. This work clearly represents Meredith's attempt to transmute into art the pangs of jealousy, misery, rage and guilt attendant on the collapse of his relationship with Mary Ellen.

It seems ironic that an author who wished to be valued 'by that in my poetry which emphasizes the unity of life, the soul that breathes through the universe'[9] should be chiefly remembered for a work about alienation. But 'Modern Love' is not such an aberration as is sometimes suggested.[10] The couple's problems are set against the same natural and emotional landscape as that established in the earlier love poetry – which is precisely what makes them so painful for the husband. He can no longer 'endow / With spiritual splendour a white brow' or be transported by the 'great flood' of his passion (ML XXIX). As much as anything else Meredith ever wrote, the sequence deals with man's place in nature and with how, anticipating his later verse, to 'read aright / Her meaning' ('Hard Weather'). Most importantly, the poet's vision of an overarching relationship between nature and man is queried but reaffirmed. He comes to see, as always in his mature work, that the problem lies with human folly, not with nature itself: 'More brain, O Lord, more brain!' cries the husband, from whose point of view most of the sequence is written, 'or we shall mar / Utterly this fair garden we might win' (ML XLVIII).

The opening sonnet immediately draws attention to the danger. It shows a couple in their marriage bed – or 'marriage-tomb' as the narrator puts it, already expressing his despair in their future together, and foreshadowing the tragedy to come.

Shakespeare's sonnet sequence also opens with the threat of the grave, to urge procreation as a means of defying time; here, the threat seems much more painfully imminent. The wife is racked by sobs, which overwhelm her suddenly, and which she tries to smother. The sounds, 'strangled mute, like little gaping snakes' pierce her husband to the quick. Their paradise has indeed been invaded, and the title, along with the marriage to which it refers, is at once revealed as a sham. The couple's love has not actually gone; they suffer for each other as well as for themselves. But it has changed, and is far from what it once was. It is hard now to imagine the impact of this disturbing scene on a readership whose last glimpse of the marital bed in poetry may have been Frederick Graham kissing his loyal wife's 'kind warm neck that slept' in Coventry Patmore's *Faithful for Ever* (1860).[11] Indeed, Meredith himself adopts a strategy for distancing the pain, and examining it more objectively: the husband and wife are initially seen from the outside, as if their plight is being enacted both for him and for us, as audience, on a stage. When sending some proofs to Maxse, he even referred to it in such a way, using the title, 'A Tragedy of Modern Love' (*Letters* I: 128).

One mechanism for this objectivity soon proves unfeasible. By ML III, the narrator has begun to yield to, or merge with, the husband, who cries as if he is both at once, 'See that I am drawn to her even now!' At the end of ML IV, the narrator questions the point of looking analytically at such experiences since 'wisdom never comes when it is gold'. Soon, the effort, or rather the pretence, of his own detachment is more or less abandoned. 'Behold me' he repeats in ML VI, indicating again that the intense frustration he describes is his own, but still beckoning us to watch. Little has happened here: the narrator has simply shown the wife responding with downcast eyes to a kiss on the forehead, a gesture not so much 'chanced', as he claims, but premeditated in ML III as a way of testing her. Her unresponsiveness has therefore been enough to turn him into a furious, humiliated Othello: 'Dead! Is it dead!' he cries in his own voice, apparently referring to their love, but echoing the tragic hero's words over the dying Desdemona.[12] Clearly, he speaks for himself now:

> She has a pulse, and flow
> Of tears, the price of blood-drops, as I know,

> For whom the midnight sobs around Love's ghost,
> Since then I heard her, and so will sob on.
>
> (ML VI)

These are difficult lines. Does 'whom' refer to wife or husband? Is 'midnight' used as noun or adjective? Is 'sobs' a singular form of the verb or a plural noun? Is 'I' really the subject of 'sob on'? The would-be close reader is baffled. Is Meredith *intentionally* showing muddled thought processes?[13] This view seems too charitable. From this confusion, however, comes one certain fact, that the wife's early silent weeping still distresses the husband, even when, as the last lines here reveal, the two are sitting by the fire in apparent good humour. Involved in the same misery, from this point onwards the husband tells us his own tale. The third person narrative reappears only when he withdraws from the action again, notably at the end.

Key events in the action differ from Meredith's own experiences, and to this extent neither the husband nor this more aloof *alter ego* can properly be identified with the author. Yet part of the sonnets' effectiveness does lie in what we experience as an autobiographical intensity, just as it does in the case of another famous earlier sonnet sequence, Sidney's *Astrophil and Stella,* where the speaker says: 'I am not I: pitie the tale of me'.[14] Perhaps this is because the husband is very much a Meredithian *figure* – the spirited male whose posturings are laid bare and debunked in the hard school of life.

The probing continues. The woman seems at first to be the guilty party. But has she ever really been unfaithful? The echoes of *Othello* suggest otherwise. For all his rage and jealousy, when the husband asks himself what has gone wrong with their marriage, he finds himself at least as much at fault. He confesses to us that he assumed his wife's loyalty while he pursued his own ends: 'My crime is, that the puppet of a dream, / I plotted to be worthy of the world' (ML X). Of course, he speaks partly defensively: surely we are meant to think that 'to be worthy of the world' is not an ignoble aim. All the same, he should not have taken his wife's loyalty for granted. He should have realized that feelings change: 'I play for Seasons; not Eternities! / Says Nature, laughing on her way'. This might seem unkind of Nature, but he tells himself that it is not:

> For she the laws of growth most deeply knows,
> Whose hands bear, here, a seed-bag – there an urn.
> Pledged she herself to aught, 'twould mark her end!
> This lesson of our only visible friend,
> Can we not teach our foolish hearts to learn?
>
> (ML XIII)

The 'for ever of a kiss' is an illusion, then (ML XIII); he has not understood this before. This whole experience is a learning process for him. That is one reason why, as Gillian Beer points out, the poems are not 'gloomy', but 'exhilarated, witty, mordant'.[15] The husband is, in an odd way, on top form, fully alive, keenly perceptive. He realizes something else now: how little he and his wife understand each other. For example, when he seeks out the 'gold-haired lady' of ML XIV as a mere diversion, he notes that his wife seems jealous in her turn. Surprised to find that women 'still may love whom they deceive', he says bitterly: 'Madam you teach me many things that be'. For his own part, he realizes that this kind of attachment, as to a possession, is not the kind of love that he can value. Here are new insights, hard won, and passed on to the reader. The sequence provides a learning experience for us as well.

Vine Cottage on Lower Halliford Green, the Merediths' deceptively idyllic base during the last period of their marriage (photograph by the present author)

Wary of direct confrontation, the couple now embark on a dangerous game. In public, they keep up a united front. The little scenes in which they do so are again staged for us, vividly dramatic rather than novelistic. Whereas once the two had secluded themselves as lovers, now they mingle with other guests at a house party, even flattering each other publicly at dinner. Nothing could be more unlike the heartfelt compliments given in Edmund Spenser's well-known courtship sonnets, the *Amoretti*. The husband labels this new game in ominous capitals, 'HIDING THE SKELETON' (ML XVII).[16] The deception distresses them both, but with different results. The husband seeks relief in sensuality. We watch him as he in turns watches some rural merrymaking on the nearby green, envying the revellers: 'Nature they seem near', he thinks, remembering that he too once seemed 'near' Nature. This brings to mind, he says, a 'country lass' he had adored, an 'early goddess' (ML XVIII; Meredith may have had in mind the girl who inspired 'Love in the Valley'). This is perilous territory: he shows his thoughts turning more purposefully to other women. Recognizing that the villagers have probably been drinking, and disdaining a 'holier than thou' attitude, he admits:

> I am not of those miserable males
> Who sniff at vice, and daring not to snap,
> Do therefore hope for heaven. I take the hap
> Of all my deeds.
>
> (ML XX)

With more than a little masculine swagger, he congratulates himself for his manly courage in sampling temptations, and accepting the consequences. At the end of ML XX, coming upon evidence of past indiscretions (a 'wanton-scented tress / in an old desk'), he confesses that there is a double standard for men and women: 'If for those times I must ask charity, / Have I not any charity to give?' But the insight yields no results; he says nothing, letting his own inclinations lead him where they will. Meanwhile, he tells us, the wife suffers too, and the cost of repressing her feeling is high. When, 'on the cedar-shadowed lawn', the pair again act the happily married couple, congratulating a friend who is newly in love, she suddenly faints. Rather than being a symptom of 'happy things' to come, this is evidently a warning: when she revives, 'her long moist hand clings mortally' to her husband's (ML XXI).

Alone together, the couple drop their pretence. Allotted a cosy 'attic-crib' at another gathering in a country house (ML XXIII), they find the forced intimacy agonizing. Astonishingly for this mid-Victorian period, this incident is described for us in almost graphic detail. The husband is not invited into the narrow bed, even though his wife is obviously awake when he comes in. He sleeps on the floor, tortured by shame and hurt pride, thinking of the little creatures suffering, even dying ('[t]he small bird stiffens') outside in the freezing night – a tacit acknowledgement of suffering shared with them because of the changing seasons in human life, as in nature. He admits this kinship again when he recalls his wife rejecting a French novel about a love triangle: 'You think it quite unnatural', he says, adding: 'Unnatural? My dear, these things are life' (ML XXV). The husband's bitterness here suggests a spiritual crisis which is colouring his whole view of existence.[17]

This bitterness allows him to act on his most selfish instincts, although he hates himself for doing so. Warning his wife in ML XXVI that he will inflict pain on her in return ('be no coward: – you that made Love bleed, / You must bear all the venom of his tooth!'), he shows himself now deliberately looking elsewhere for his satisfaction. There have already been touches of grim humour in the discrepancies between the couple's outward demeanour and inner feelings. Now there is sharp irony: 'Is the devil's line / Of golden hair, or raven black, composed?...No matter, so I taste forgetfulness' (ML XXVII). This is not the dilemma explored in Shakespeare's sonnets, even though the reference to them is unmistakable, making this a prime example of intertextuality in the sequence. The impact here comes not from similarity but from contrast: the husband's choice is not between two people loved in different ways, but between alternative possible distractions. The end decision could hardly matter less. Worse still, as the husband knows full well, he has baser motives than merely to forget what is happening in his marriage – namely, to punish his wife, and to boost his self-esteem. 'I must shine / Envied', he says imperiously, but, quite clearly, self-mockingly. Recognizing how unworthy such sentiments are, he confesses to feeling lessened in his 'proper sight'

(ML XXVIII). He is ripe, it seems, for a punishment of his own. Predictably, when he takes up with the 'gold-haired lady' already mentioned in ML XIV, he finds physical involvement, without 'the ancient wealth wherein I clothed / Our human nakedness', more disturbing than satisfying: 'Something more than earth / I cry for still: I cannot be at peace / In having Love upon a mortal lease' (ML XXIX). Chastened, he turns to nature again, this time swapping bitterness for stoicism. He has to accept the loss of his youthful passion, he tells himself – and us. The change is inevitable, natural, part of the larger picture of human existence. The scientific approach to life is vindicated. We are 'First, animals'. With its attack on the concept of romantic love as timeless, ML XXX, which is specifically addressed to the Lady rather than his wife ('Madam'), is as severely anti-Petrarchan as Shakespeare's sonnets to his Dark Lady. Again, our recognition of this adds immeasurably to the effect.

The husband's misgivings about his new relationship grow. Feeling himself 'approved', admired for his attributes ('Some women like a young philosopher', ML XXXI) rather than loved, he suddenly pictures himself in the position of a lap-dog being petted or an ornament being exhibited. The reference here is apparently to the brilliant little Polish dwarf, 'Count' Borowlaski, whose wife was said to have shown him off by putting him up on the mantelpiece.[18] He fears a falling-off of integrity, something that he finds suggested in Raphael's resplendently over-feathered St Michael in 'St Michael and the Devil' in the Louvre; or a loss of manliness, this time exemplified by the undisciplined soldiers fighting for Pompey at the Battle of Pharsalia (ML XXXIII). Once he had hoped to be envied as the 'God of such a grand sunflower', a desire which even then had made him look ridiculous in his own eyes (ML XXVIII). Now he finds his ego diminished rather than bolstered by his liaison. We realize that the affair has indeed become one of his self-administered scourgings.

This long winter is not yet over. Supposing him happy with the other woman, his wife finally tries to speak to him in ML XXXIV; their 'chain on silence clanks'. But, part comically and part tragically, the husband pretends to be immersed in his journals and refuses to be 'melted', warding off a show-down with 'commonplace' responses. The contrast with the coyly domestic scenes of Patmore's work could not be greater. The wife is so vulnerable now that the impasse between them seems certain to end in floods of tears or a violent eruption: Niagara or Vesuvius, as the husband admits, is only 'deferred'. When their silence resumes in ML XXXV, he finds it more stressful than ever: 'O have a care of natures that are mute! / They punish you in acts', he says with epigrammatic terseness. Their next close encounter is a kiss imposed during a game of forfeits in the snow. His 'Lady' is also present at this gathering, and he views the two women's exchange of compliments with incredulity. The house party continues with the wonderfully evocative evening scene of ML XXXVII, and he remains preternaturally aware of both women. While some of the older guests on the garden terrace, immune to the beauty of the glimmering valley below them, wait impatiently to be summoned to dinner ('grey seniors question Time / In irritable coughings'), he puzzles over this strange situation: 'Our tragedy, is it alive or dead?' he asks. On this same occasion, it seems, his Lady finally gives herself to him – only for 'this heavenly tune' to be marred when he glimpses his wife with another man, and observes their hands touching (ML XXXIX). He has the answer to his question, then: the tragedy continues to play itself out. 'The dread that my old love may be alive, / Has seized my nursling new love by the throat' (ML XL), he reports.

The climax comes when, unable to throw off the hold of their shared past, the husband and wife agree to relinquish their new relationships, and commit themselves to each other again. They do so without enthusiasm: 'O, look we like a pair / Who for fresh nuptials joyfully yield all else?' (ML XLI) asks the husband grimly. Inevitably then their lovemaking is far from joyful, vitiated not only by his own mixed feelings but also by the wife's certainty that his heart is given elsewhere, and that he merely pities her. Yet, poignantly, in the midst of such high emotional drama, and even as the final disaster approaches, the two stroll by the river together on an autumn evening, feeling momentarily at one with the world:

> We saw the swallows gathering in the sky,
> And in the osier-isle we heard them noise.
> We had not to look back on summer joys,
> Or forward to a summer of bright dye:

> But in the largeness of the evening earth
> Our spirits grew as we went side by side.
> The hour became her husband and my bride.
> Love, that had robbed us so, thus blessed our dearth!
> The pilgrims of the year waxed very loud
> In multitudinous chatterings, as the flood
> Full brown came from the West, and like pale blood
> Expanded to the upper crimson cloud.
> Love, that had robbed us of immortal things,
> This little moment mercifully gave,
> Where I have seen across the twilight wave
> The swan sail with her young beneath her wings.
>
> (ML XLVII)

Glimpsed on the garden terrace in ML XXXVII, this is the 'heavenly tune' marred when he was with the Lady in ML XXXIX. Disappointed both in youthful passion for his wife, and the mere 'game of Sentiment' with the Lady (ML XXVIII), the husband is not after all disappointed in nature. He has learnt the important lesson at last – to live in the present. The verb here (in 'We had not to look back on summer joys, / Or forward to a summer of bright dye') is best read not as a simple past tense, but as indicating what was required, what they 'had' to do for their souls to expand. Only when neither looking back nor looking forward were they able, briefly, to achieve harmony with each other and with the beauty around them. Paradoxically, the sonnet is full of references to the passing of time and season, from swallows gathering in the evening air to the swan once seen in the same spot, protecting her cygnets beneath her wings. In the colour of the water rising to meet the sunset ('pale blood' against 'crimson'), the pain caused by this inevitable passage is also suggested. But the 'little moment' they share together is perfect, timeless and infinitely precious.

Open to each other at last, the husband and wife talk frankly, asking questions and laying bare their feelings. Ironically, this provokes the tragic ending. Meredith would famously say in Part IV of 'The Woods of Westermain' (1883), 'Blood and brain and spirit, three.../Join for true felicity'; but here, at this crucial point, 'brain', or the ability to understand each other properly, is lacking. The wife acts on the 'jealous devotion' roused by her husband's confession and decides to set him free by taking a potion. This is a tragedy in the true, Aristotelian sense. The husband recognizes his wife's selflessness: while hating what she has done, 'I do adore the nobleness!' he cries (ML XLVIII); the narrator, reappearing here, is saddened by their later struggles, and salvages memories of their early happiness: 'Lovers beneath the singing sky of May, / They wandered once; clear as the dew on flowers'; while the final message, continuing from the narrator's reminiscence but extrapolated from the story as a whole, is that there is no certainty in this world except change itself, and that man must have the courage to accept this and feed 'on the advancing hours' (ML L).

The much discussed imagery in the concluding sentence, of breakers advancing on the shore like 'ramping hosts of warrior horse' and throwing a 'faint thin' line on the margin, suggests the cosmic forces that impinge on our lives. Reminiscent of the imagery used in 'The Shipwreck of Idomeneus', and also in some verses that Meredith gave Janet Duff Gordon, in which he likens waves to 'phantom hosts of warrior horse' (*SL*, 33), it indicates that the protagonists' struggle is representative: they too have been subject to this dynamic flux, even though the husband acknowledged it, and drew strength from knowing it, only fleetingly. Hardly 'predictably pious',[19] such an ending does invest their personal crisis with a consoling universality. This reading is confirmed by 'The Promise in Disturbance', the new tightly-rhymed, fourteen-line sonnet with which Meredith prefaced the sequence when it was reprinted in 1892. Here, he asks the reader to discern beyond the 'jangled strain' intimations of a larger harmony, 'a newly-added chord, / Commanding space beyond where ear has home'.[20]

Only Shakespeare's Dark Lady sonnets plumb the same depths of emotional, psychological and spiritual turmoil as 'Modern Love'. But there the relationship concerned is outside marriage. Here, playing off against earlier sonneteers, Meredith has called into question not simply the romantic yearnings of courtly love, but, much more shockingly for his contemporaries, the ideal of conjugal bliss to which Spenser's sonnet sequence had tended. In place of the 'timely fruit' prayed for by the narrator of that poet's *Epithalamion*, Meredith offers in ML XI a lurid image of the crescent moon cradling a 'dead infant'. This represents graphically the havoc wrought on the unfortunate pair's chance of fulfilment together. No wonder some early reviewers found the sequence repugnant: 'In "Modern Love" we have disease, and nothing else', wrote J. W. Marston in the *Athenaeum* (*CH*, 101); 'a sickly little peccadillo' muttered an anonymous contributor to the *Saturday Review* (*CH*, 106). But Meredith's candour would eventually be appreciated. By 1909 even a man of the cloth, the Rev. James Moffat, could describe the work as a 'searching and poignant sequence of poems' (*CH*, 499). Now, in its frankness, complication of feelings and narration, its liberty with the sonnet form and its relation to previous sonnet cycles, it can be recognized as pioneering. But its greatest triumph lies in Meredith's involving us so powerfully both in the struggle to face and face down human weakness, and in that 'little moment' when the 'largeness of the world' opens up to us.

3

The First 'Thwackings': From *The Shaving of Shagpat* to *The Adventures of Harry Richmond*

Meredith would not publish another volume of verse for over twenty years. To support himself and his family, he needed to write novels, sometimes having two or three on hand at once. Here too he struggled to be true to himself and his grand vision of life, and (in every sense) raise a readership.

THE EARLY FANTASIES

In his earliest prose works, he had followed the 'vagaries of his own brain', as he put it to Jessopp (*Letters* I: 160). *The Shaving of Shagpat* and *Farina* both take their heroes on extraordinary journeys to fulfil seemingly impossible missions, which reveal their (and our) human limitations and powers. The first and more engaging of these two fantasies, inspired partly by the outlandish tale heard at the Duff Gordons, partly also by the age-old myth of strength residing in hair, *The Shaving of Shagpat* is as exuberant as the early poems, and with little of their self-imposed formal constraint.

Shibli Bagarag's mission is to shave off the 'Identical', the one special hair on the enormously bushy head of the clothier Shagpat that makes everyone kowtow to him. In the kind of fusion of the real and the surreal now dubbed magic realism, Shibli is as endearingly ordinary as his task is extraordinary. Reminiscent of his creator, he strides along hopefully, 'brushing among the flowers and soft mosses of the meadows, lifting his nostrils to the joyful smells, looking about him with the broad eye of one that hungereth for a coming thing'. Easily carried away by his own pride, in this same episode he manages to catch the treacherous Horse Garraveen, only to ignore the instruction to dismount. The result is an ignominious ducking in the water-meadows, one of the physical 'thwackings' that his inflated ego invites. 'Leave me not my betrothed', he begs the mysterious old crone he has promised to marry, Noorna bin Noorka, for 'what am I without thy counsel?' (*SS*, 'The Horse Garraveen'; 134, 137). Yet in contrast to the youth in the interpolated tale about Bhanavar the Beautiful, Shibli succeeds in his mission. Having become, in Meredith's sharp, memorable terminology, 'The Master of the Event', he is rewarded when Noorna turns into his beautiful young bride. With its high-flown style, snippets of rollicking verse, seasoning of humour, and opportunities for allegorical interpretation, the fantasy earned Meredith his first devotees. More important, it initiates us with youthful panache into the Meredithian project: the battle to achieve not so much mastery as *self*-mastery.

Chapman & Hall had advanced Meredith £70 for *Shagpat*, but, despite George Eliot's approving review, sales were poor and he had to find another publisher for *Farina*. Brought out by Smith, Elder & Co., the new tale is set in medieval Rhineland, and mixes swashbuckling action with supernatural and scientific elements. Again, the hero needs help from outside, a common state of affairs in Meredith's novels. In this case, the young scientist Farina is outshone by his new friend Guy de Goshawk, a bluff Englishman with elements of Robin Hood, Richard the Lionheart, and (it seems) Meredith himself. The main action recalls the Robin Hood stories, since it involves rescuing Farina's beloved Margarita from the clutches of a wicked baron – though with the additional help of a more fanciful Lorelei-figure called the 'Water-Lady'. Walter Crane caught both the flavour and weakness of the narrative in his design for the title page of the 1865 edition, showing Guy, the epitome of the chivalric ideal, astride the fallen baron, with one arm protectively around Margarita as she gazes lovingly into the eyes of a puny Farina. Only when the defeated baron's champion, none other than the devil himself, pollutes the city with a poisonous stench, does Farina come into his own: he produces a new distillation, *eau de Cologne*, to purify the air. But nothing is made of the conquest of evil by natural essences;[1] and, having won Margarita for himself, Farina is left dependent on 'his sweet young bride, leading him from snares, priming his soul with celestial freshness' (*F*, Conclusion; 120). Olde worlde archaisms and a flurry of interjections like 'Devil's Breeches!' and 'Thousand Thunders!' fail to engage us in what one reviewer called, with some justification, 'a trifling subject' (*CH*, 52).

Meredith would always veer towards the fabulous and the 'epical' (*Letters* I: 323). The expansiveness of his personality was not to be denied; it is one of his attractions as a writer. But now he would try to reach out to 'the *heart* of the mass' (*Letters* I: 160). Shibli's challenges had not been presented as mere picaresque adventures, but as tests of character, administered with a purpose: Noorna upbraids him when he groans after being beaten by Shagpat's wife, 'What! thou hast been thwacked, and refusest the fruit of it – which is resoluteness, strength of mind, sternness in pursuit of the object!' (*SS*, 'The Thwackings', 13). Now, Meredith would confront his heroes with more convincing obstacles, provoked by their own characters, and reveal their inner lives through their responses to them. Realizing that the necessary adjustment to society on the one hand, and the enlargement of the spirit on the other, can only come from within, he would investigate and encourage *us* to investigate the process of maturing more thoroughly. The Bildungsroman, a form which he probably encountered while at Neuwied, turned out to be best for this task, though he was never confined by it.[2] His two most significant earlier novels adapt as much as adopt it: *The Ordeal of Richard Feverel*, written before 'Modern Love', and *The Adventures of Harry Richmond*, written at the end of the 1860s.

THE ORDEAL OF RICHARD FEVEREL

Possibly Chapman & Hall had held back from *Farina* to bring out the other, more ambitious novel Meredith was working on.[3] If so, they chose well: daringly explicit and heart-wrenching, *The Ordeal of Richard Feverel* is the work with which he first challenged the literary establishment. Despite its two predecessors it is often treated as an autobiographical first novel, and no doubt it derives much of its power from its author's own 'ordeal', still in unhappy progress during much of the writing. But here, in advance of 'Modern Love', he does what Milan Kundera says all good novelists do – 'destroys the house of his life and uses its stones to build the house of his novel'.[4] For, while the narrative revolves around the relationships between father and son, and husband and wife, the fundamental concern is with the wider picture, specifically, with the effort to achieve moral, intellectual and spiritual growth within the greater scheme of nature.

Meredith and Arthur, his son by Mary Ellen, in a photograph taken by William Hardman in 1862 (*A Mid-Victorian Pepys: The Letters and Memoirs of Sir William Hardman, MA FRGS* ed. S. M. Ellis (Cecil Palmer, 1923), facing p.50)

Unfortunately, Sir Austin Feverel has taken it upon himself to oversee this growth in his only son. Embittered by his wife's having left him for his protégé, a poet with the unappealing pen-name of Diaper Sandoe,[5] he decides to shelter young Richard from corruption and have him educated at home in Raynham Abbey. Here he will prepare 'The Hope of Raynham' for a grand future and, going further than other protective parents in Victorian fiction,[6] shield him from women until he finds him a suitable partner at what he considers a suitable age – 30, in the first edition of the novel, later relaxed to 25. Sir Austin's 'System', similar to that recommended in Rousseau's *Émile*, might have commended itself to contemporary readers, especially since it is imbued with the pre-Darwinian thinking of Herbert Spencer: Richard is seen as a 'living Tree' with its seasons (*ORF* 12; 100).[7] But Meredith quickly makes us aware of fundamental problems with it. Given to hitting off ideas and setting them in stone as aphorisms, Sir Austin is not only embittered but stubbornly blinkered.[8] As the boy's tutor he selects his nephew Adrian Harley, a rotund epicure with a bad digestion, a cynic like himself. This 'Wise Youth' is shown to lack natural sympathies and even sound values; he is the nearest thing to an evil character in the whole novel.[9] More fundamentally, as Adrian himself is allowed to point out to us, Sir Austin's subconscious motive is 'to be Providence to his son' (*ORF* 4; 35); and life, especially as Meredith sees it, punishes such presumption. The devotion of another of Richard's cousins, Clare, and of Ripton Thompson, Sir Austin's solicitor's son, is patently problematic too, encouraging Richard to believe he is destined for great things. The stage is early set for a catalogue of disasters, and a tragic denouement involving father, son and all those close to them.

Richard first rebels against the 'System' in his early teens, when he and Ripton are whipped for poaching by Farmer Blaize. Accustomed to the rod, 'Rip', we note, soon gets over it; 'the Young Experiment' does not. Burning with the indignity of it, he externalizes his emotions by paying a yeoman to fire the farmer's ricks. In the end, by insisting on going alone to the farmhouse to set things right, he emerges well from this 'Preliminary Ordeal' (*ORF* 10; heading). But it forges a link in an ominous chain. The yeoman becomes another of Richard's devotees; as his groom, Tom Bakewell will one day aid and abet his master's secret marriage. First, though, comes another push against the 'System'. In later adolescence, Richard indulges in versifying. Diaper Sandoe has not endeared poets to Sir Austin, who finds this unmanly practice less acceptable than boyish high spirits. Our hearts go out to Richard as he reluctantly consigns his 'neatly tied, named, and numbered' bundles of poems to the fire (*ORF* 12; 102). Again the problem is resolved; but not without damage to the father–son relationship. Worse, the youth's overheated feelings lose their outlet. Richard has now entered the 'Magnetic Age: the Age of violent attractions' (*ORF* 13; 102). Suddenly, the real ordeal is upon him. He had barely noticed Farmer Blaize's pretty niece before, but when he sees Lucy Desborough now, '[s]urrounded by the green shaven meadows, the pastoral summer buzz, the weirfall's thundering white, amid the breath and beauty of wild flowers' (*ORF* 14; 119), it is a different matter. In this setting, at once reminiscent of Thames-side Shepperton and paradisiacal, Lucy is an unfallen Eve, 'the First Woman to him' (*ORF* 15; 120). She is also, in another analogy, Miranda to his Ferdinand. Both analogies work on us, but neither carries through completely. The fall predicted here comes about through Richard, not Lucy; and Meredith soon shows that Sir Austin's manipulations are far from those of a wise Prospero.

A farmer's niece was never part of the latter's plan for Richard, an added complication being that this one is a Catholic. Both Adrian and Lady Blandish, Sir Austin's widowed friend and neighbour, are duly employed to deal with her. She should give him up, they tell her, for Richard's own good. The reader, already a sympathetic spectator, now finds a representative in Lady Blandish, who takes to the girl, convinced of the genuineness of her feelings. This kindly woman writes to Sir Austin, assuring him that their interview bore fruit, but adding cryptically, 'Are we so bad?...I hope I have really been doing right!' She goes on to raise uncomfortable but vague questions about the need to be 'sure of one's cause' and the advisability of inspecting 'the machinery of wisdom', subtly challenging his infallibility with an aphorism of her own ('When a wise man makes a false step, will he not go farther than a fool?'), and by remarks on the egotism of Gibbon and other great writers (*ORF*

22; 191–2). Meredith hints not only at her reservations, but at Sir Austin's inkling of them:

> He trifled with the letter for some time, rereading chosen passages as he walked about the room, and considering he scarce knew what. There are ideas language is too gross for, and shape too arbitrary, which come to us and have a definite influence upon us, and yet we cannot fasten on the filmy things and make them visible and distinct to ourselves, much more to others. Why did he twice throw a look into the glass in the act of passing it? Why did he for a moment stand with erect head facing it?

Sir Austin scrutinizes himself carefully, 'as one who looks at this essential self through the mask we wear'. But, in the end, neither his reflection nor his reflections tell him anything worthwhile. It is left to the narrator to remark cynically on his lack of a sense of humour: 'a good wind of laughter had relieved him of much of the blight of self-deception, and oddness, and extravagance; had given a healthier view of our atmosphere of life: but he had it not' (*ORF* 22; 193–5). Sir Austin is wrong to interfere in the young couple's relationship. We can see this; but, without such a corrective, Sir Austin cannot.

All Meredith is here already in embryo: his faith in the greater sensitivity of women; his concern with the elusiveness of meaning and the need to read intelligently; his sense of our larger context ('our atmosphere of life'); and his conviction, directly relayed to us, that self-importance and self-deception must be swept away by the comic principle – an idea to be fully explored later in his *Essay on Comedy*.

As it is, Sir Austin sails on, unenlightened. Richard's dutiful letters to him from London, when he is arranging his wedding, strike his father as 'rather monotonous and spiritless', but arouse no suspicion in him. On the contrary: 'The letters of a healthful physique!' he crows, thinking Richard has got over the 'Apple Disease' exhibited by his wayward first love. Again, the narrator himself points out the irony here: 'Complacently he sat and smiled, little witting that his son's ordeal was imminent and that his son's ordeal was to be his own' (*ORF* 28; 283).

The couple marry. From following the consecutive 'seasons' of Richard's youth Meredith now shows the newly-weds being tested separately in two interconnected melodramas. Tricked into leaving his bride, and exposed to the temptations of city life, Richard is endangered by the very idealism that the 'System' has nurtured in him. Naively casting himself as the champion of fallen women, he gets Ripton to track down his mother, and extricates her somewhat reluctantly from her dishonourable relationship; and he consorts with Bella Mount, once the mistress of a certain Lord Mountfalcon. Much as his old nursemaid Mrs Berry has led us to fear, he ends up betraying his 'dear home-angel' with Bella (*ORF* 43; 526). Lucy, on the other hand, stays loyal, despite the blandishments of the wealthy Mountfalcon himself. Sir Austin, however, still feeling betrayed by his son's secret marriage, is fatally slow to appreciate her worth and welcome her to Raynham Abbey. And Richard, already too ashamed to return to her, receives another blow to his self-esteem. His cousin Clare commits suicide, and, from reading her diary, he realises finally what we have guessed all along, that she had loved him, and that his cavalier treatment of her had crushed her spirit.[10] Like his father, Richard has helped make a tragedy out of the 'New Comedy' – parents' conflict with their children over the choice of marriage partners. Yearning to cleanse himself, he sets off for the Continent.

Has Richard learnt as much about himself as we have? Not yet. Despite noticing his Austrian contemporaries' steady, useful lives ('Not cloud-work theirs!'), he again sees himself in some splendidly heroic role – helping to liberate Italy, no less. 'Had he not been nursed to believe he was born for great things?' (*ORF* 42; 515–16). To our dismay, he continues, quite deliberately, to detach himself from reality, destroying letters from home unread lest they should persuade him to return, his sins unexpunged. Only when another cousin, the kind and sensible Austin Wentworth, comes out and reveals his fatherhood to him does his mind begin to clear. In a well-known episode, Richard walks in a forest in the Rhineland during a drenching storm, picks up a leveret, and feels it licking his hand roughly: 'What did it say to him? Human tongue could not have said so much just then' (*ORF* 42: 522–3). Blood and spirit combine in this pre-Lawrentian epiphany, as the sensation is reinforced by the sight of a simple woodland shrine with figures of the Madonna and Child. Richard knows himself part of the vital onward sweep of life at last, and sets out for home, Lucy and his son.

At this juncture, another novelist might have stopped. But no one, certainly not the reader, is to escape the havoc wrought by the 'System'. At his London hotel, Richard picks up an old message from Bella, telling him of her discovery that she had been actively deployed to distract him while Mountfalcon laid siege to Lucy. She had urged him to return to his wife, as he is now doing. But, like his father before him, Richard reads poorly. The letter only serves to divert him again: the flame of his enlightenment in the forest gutters, and his exaggerated sense of honour propels him to challenge Mountalcon to a duel. We see him being sucked back into melodrama, leaving Lucy traumatized, as all hope of a happy ending fades. The joyful reunion at Raynham becomes a poignant leave-taking before the dangerous appointment. Meredith really does seem, in Virginia Woolf's words, intent on destroying 'the conventional form of the novel' (Norton, 533).

Then, in a further assault on convention, the narrative ends inconclusively, with another letter. Lady Blandish reports to Austin Wentworth that Richard was wounded, and that Sir Austin barred Lucy from ministering to him, insisting that she attend to her infant son – his precious grandchild – instead. For Lucy, the strain has been too great: her natural urges cruelly baulked, she has died of that old malady, brain fever. Now, Lady Blandish continues, Richard himself is recovering, but has received the news as a 'death-blow to his heart' and will 'never be what he promised' (*ORF* 45; 557).

In this entirely credible, catastrophic outcome, the two innocent, vulnerable young women who loved Richard have died, and both the father and son on whom the narrative focuses are left devastated. Like Lady Blandish we feel inclined to lay all the blame at Sir Austin's door. He had ignored the doubts she raised, and embraced rather than struggled against his own obstinacy. Now, we too fear that he is impervious to life's lessons, and might try to inflict the 'System' on his grandson. Worse still is the suspicion that nature itself is implicated in all this. Had Richard not inherited his father's inflexibility? And what could have been more 'natural' than his behaviour with Bella? As Mrs Berry says when talking about her own philandering husband: 'what [young men] goes and does they ain't quite answerable for: they feels, I dare say, pushed from behind' (*ORF* 41; 511). As in 'Modern Love', we are left with an ending seemingly tainted by despair over the human condition.

Yet, again, there are sparks of hope, principally Richard's illumination by the 'Spirit of Life' in the Rhineland (*ORF* 42; 523), and, linked to that, the very existence of the infant, testifying to nature's continuing processes. And in Mrs Berry's sturdy philosophy, at least, Providence still operates: 'I think it's al'ays the plan in a dielemmer to pray God and walk forward' (*ORF* 40; 491). Also to be noted is Lady Blandish's purpose in writing to Austin Wentworth. Richard has asked for him – a promising sign. She herself wants his help, to reconcile her with the older Austin. As incontrovertibly good-hearted as Mrs Berry,[11] this younger man can be depended upon to help them both. Not merely a 'dazzling solution to the technical problem ...of bringing a narrative to an end' with a more sympathetic voice than the narrator's,[12] Lady Blandish's letter provides the last scene of an action on which the curtain has yet to fall, and which still has possibilities for change and growth. Having gone through Richard's ordeal with him, we are left to consider what these possibilities might be, both in the characters' lives and in our own.

NOVELS OF THE 1860s

In *Richard Feverel*, Meredith had woven together various narrative modes (the picaresque and the heroic; romance and melodrama); forms (aphorisms, poetry, letters and Clare's diary entries); and tones (comic as well as tragic, the two meeting uneasily in the Dickensian Mrs Berry). Now he began to tease out some of the threads for fuller treatment. Heredity and class issues are dealt with next, in *Evan Harrington*, the story of a tailor's son who falls in love with and wins the well-born Rose Jocelyn. Meredith then developed the more impressive heroine of *Sandra Belloni* and its sequel *Vittoria*, a woman capable of involving herself in the kind of heroics Richard Feverel had only, and foolishly, dreamt of in Europe. In between these two novels, and written concurrently with the latter, came his shorter social problem novel, *Rhoda Fleming*, taking up Richard's earlier cause – the championing of fallen women, but in a rural context.

The most entertaining is the first. Written after his separation from Mary Ellen, and in hopes of a new start with young Janet Duff Gordon, *Evan Harrington* is a fairly conventional romance on a theme close to Meredith's heart: that a lowly background need be no bar to marrying into the upper classes. Curiously for one so evasive about his origins, Meredith brings in various family members and other people from his Portsmouth childhood, including his bombastic tailoring grandfather, without even changing their names.[13] The 'Great Mel' is presented as Evan's father, who has just died when the novel opens, a fact that does little to lessen the impression this 'efflorescence of sublime imposture' makes on us (*EH* 20; 257). His presence is felt partly through memories and gossip, but most distinctly through the pretensions of his youngest daughter – Evan's snobbish sister, the equally unforgettable Countess of Saldar. When her socially insecure brother returns briefly to his father's profession, she is outraged; as for his having shaved off his moustache: 'Why, mon Dieu!' she cries, 'one could hardly tell you, as you look now, from the very commonest tradesman'. She follows this, quite inconsequentially, by expressing her feelings about hair loss in women: 'Oh horror! total extinction is better than to rise again in a wig!' (*EH* 9; 104–5).Yet she is by no means ridiculous. Referred to as the General, she is a strategist of the first order, stopping at nothing to prop up her pretensions. She even passes herself off as the daughter of a certain conveniently deceased Sir Abraham Harrington. It is perfectly clear from this novel alone that Meredith accepts Darwinism in principle: the Countess and her siblings all carry traits from both their parents 'hereditarily combined' (*EH* 3; 19).[14] But this does not stop him making humorous capital here of the contemporary debate over ancestry and evolution, something he does most blatantly through the clever mimicry of Jacko, the Great Mel's pet monkey.

Evan Harrington too ends with a letter, but since it is written by the Countess, it is not to be taken seriously. Evan, she reports to her sister Caroline, has not only won his bride but is now serving as an attaché in Naples. Thus he has become a gentleman indeed, whom she need no longer be ashamed to acknowledge. Incorrigibly designing, the 'General' now turns her attention to Caroline's own future, with a promise to find her 'a Roman prince' (*EH* 47; 571). She feels sure that Providence is on her side, even if it answers her many requests in unexpected ways. Had such a belief been expressed in the novel by the worthy Lady Jocelyn, Evan's new mother-in-law, it would have carried weight, but here it only confirms the Countess's complacency.

Should we ask, then, as Lady Blandish does when talking of Falstaff in her first letter to Sir Austin, what all this *illustrates*? Meredith himself was dismissive of the novel: 'it is quite destitute of the *lumen purpureum* which I like to give. How a work without colour can please you at all astonishes me', he wrote to Rossetti (*Letters* I: 70). Perhaps what it shows most is that he was beginning to take his own social insecurity somewhat more lightly. At any rate, partly for its perceived superficiality, partly also perhaps because Janet Duff Gordon had now married someone else, he was keen to move on from it.

*

Rhoda Fleming is more serious than *Evan Harrington*, but unfortunately less engaging as well. For obvious reasons, Meredith's rustics are much less convincing than his 'thon of a thnip' (*EH* 44; 542). The Flemings' cook Mrs Sumfit, for instance, is another rather-too-simple soul like Mrs Berry, with whom she shares an embarrassing stock semi-illiteracy – 'gownds' for 'gowns' and so on. Even Meredith himself took every opportunity to avoid these characters, expatiating instead on countryside topics in which more educated readers might be interested, such as fox-hunting. His views are fascinating to read now. For instance, he correctly prophesied that people would one day have to hunt without real foxes. But this kind of peripheralism, as it has usefully been labelled, is distracting.[15] Worse, the heroine herself is left as a shallow and altogether ambiguous figure. At one point Rhoda even prays repeatedly for her deserted sister Dahlia to die rather than live in disgrace. No wonder she has been found 'repellent with all her virtues'.[16] Is it possible, then, that when the dying Dahlia murmurs 'Help poor girls' at the end, she is referring not only to fallen women like herself, but also to narrow-minded women like Rhoda?[17] Note that she is speaking here to Rhoda's husband Robert, with whom, we are told, she shares a 'deeper community' on the subject than with her sister (*ORF* 48; 499). Yet it seems unlikely that Meredith would have intended her words to be interpreted quite so subtly, or would have wanted to divert attention from Dahlia and her main, poignant message, at this crucial point. Perhaps such interpretations say more about later readers' expectations than Meredith's.

*

Certainly, though, Meredith was asking more and more of us now. In *Evan Harrington*, he had humoured the reader with comments like 'Pardon me, I beg' (*EH* 23; 286), or 'you will understand how it was' (*EH* 31; 398). This of course is very much in the Victorian mode. Trollope, to take just one example, often addresses the 'readers of these pages' and refers equally familiarly to this character or that as 'our friend'.[18] But Meredith's relationship with the reading public had recently had a setback: Mudie's Lending Library had felt obliged to cancel its order for *Richard Feverel* because of objections to the scenes with Bella. 'O canting Age!' he ranted. 'I am tabooed from all decent drawing-room tables' (*Letters* I: 39). In this next novel,

Emilie Maceroni (later Lady Hornby), the original of Emilia Sandra Belloni (Vittoria), from S. M. Ellis, *George Meredith: His Life and Friends in Relation to His Work* (Grant Richards: 1920, 2nd ed.), facing p.180

then, he is rather more high-handed. The narrator in *Sandra Belloni* becomes a character in his own right, arguing with another commentator, a 'garrulous, super-subtle, so-called Philosopher' who is 'blind to the fact that the public detest him' (*SB* 44; 483). Their metafictional skirmishes, though less of a feature than the Novelist and Dame Gossip's in *The Amazing Marriage*,[19] ensure that we stand back a little and employ our minds as well as our hearts in reading the narrative. Here, in particular, they set us on our guard against the Philosopher's chief bugbear, sentimentalism. The result is a heightened appreciation of Meredith's new heroine. Primed by the Philosopher, we can see how markedly Emilia Sandra contrasts with the shallow, sentimental Pole sisters and their affected, easily-swayed brother, Wilfrid. Besides being refreshingly direct, she is energetic and ardent, with all the potential to carry the planned sequel forward.

In *Vittoria*, this young woman with her beautiful voice has moved from Surrey to Milan. Here she acquires her symbolic stage name of Vittoria and becomes heavily involved in the Italian struggle for unification and independence. This narrative too starts well, with a powerful scene in which 'the Chief', Meredith's representation of Giuseppe Mazzini, is seen silhouetted against a majestic skyline. Here was a revolutionary with whose vision of life Meredith himself had much in common.[20] Other haunting passages follow. When Vittoria sings one of her old songs, for instance, it conjures up for Wilfrid (now in the Austrian army, and engaged to an Austrian woman) a magical 'vision of a foaming weir, and moonlight between the branches of a great cedar-tree, and the lost love of his heart sitting by his side in the noising stillness' (*V* 28; 348). Clearly, Meredith was aiming at maximum, unmediated impact here. He had told Jessopp, or, rather, Mrs Jessopp, to expect a blockbuster in this sequel, 'no Philosopher present: action: excitement: holding of your breath, chilling horror: classic sensation' (*Letters* I: 255).

However, we soon become lost amid 'the marches and counter-marches, the journeys, flights and returns' of the uprisings, a welter of characters, and some highly-coloured scenes of fighting (*CH*, 154). Chapters 30 to 34, for example, all concern 'Episodes of the Revolt and War'. As Meredith himself once wrote to Maxse, if there is too much plot, 'the blood of this world has no free space to circulate' (*Letters* I: 42). He had poured his heart and soul into this novel, aiming to prove that dedication to a noble cause elevates the individual to that harmony with 'heaven and the stars' for which he so yearned (*V* 21; 252). Vittoria is attractive and spirited enough, and for some patient and committed readers, he did prove it. But he found himself writing sadly to Swinburne, another enthusiastic supporter of the Italian cause and perhaps the novel's biggest fan, '"Vittoria", as I am told by Chapman and others, is not liked' (*Letters* I: 329).

THE ADVENTURES OF HARRY RICHMOND

Only with a return to the Bildungsroman, with its inbuilt impetus, could Meredith carry us along with him more readily, and involve us more deeply in the growth of his chief protagonist's inner life. Although he revised *The Adventures of Harry Richmond* before it was published in 1870 (see *SL*, 55n.), he had planned and made a start on it as early as 1864 (see *Letters* I: 250, 254), and Harry's inheritance of family traits and efforts to find his own identity, his own place in life, clearly belong with those of Richard Feverel and Evan Harrington. Like all Meredith's novels, this one is packed with incident, romantic interest and memorable characters, but, as in *Richard Feverel*, the struggle at its heart is simply to escape paternal influence, and this time the goal is much more successfully achieved.

What makes *Harry Richmond* unique among Meredith's novels, though, is the fact that it is related in the first person. Especially striking is the attempt to capture the child's-eye view at the beginning. Harry is caught between two fiery and warring figures: his wealthy maternal grandfather, Squire Beltham of Riversley Grange, and his taller, altogether more robust and colourful, even mesmerizing father, Roy Richmond. The narrative opens with their dramatic encounter at midnight, after Richmond has rung the bell and banged violently on the Squire's door like a marauder, demanding to see the wife who has deserted him. The Squire, when roused, supposes a fire to have broken out, and, figuratively speaking, he is not far wrong.[21] He passionately upbraids Richmond for having deprived his daughter of her senses. Unable to gain admittance to his wife, Richmond equally passionately lays claim to his son, who is brought to the door wretched and shivering from his warm bed. The child 'found himself facing the man of the night. It appeared to him that the stranger was of enormous size, like the giants of fairy books: for as he stood a little out of the doorway there was a peep of night sky and trees behind him, and the trees looked very much smaller, and hardly any sky was to be seen except over his shoulders' (AHR 1; 10).

Obscuring nature, Richmond almost fills the frame for Harry here and for months to come. Having snatched him away from Riversley, he takes the child with him on his travels as if on a magic carpet, with vistas opening and closing, places and figures advancing and retreating, a childhood ailment magicked away 'by smelling at an apple' (AHR 4; 40), tears and smiles equally easily provoked. That the boy grows deeply attached to him shows in another wrenching scene, when Aunt Dorothy, his mother's sister (his mother now having died), attempts to restore him to Riversley, while Mrs Waddy, his father's housekeeper, clings to him in London. Even in the absence of the two men, passions rise so high that the heat communicates itself to Harry:

> Aunt Dorothy looked at me. 'Come now', she said; 'come with me, Harry'. Her trembling seized on me like a fire. I said, 'Yes', though my heart sank as if I had lost my father with the word... We were stopped in the doorway by Mrs Waddy. Nothing could tempt her to surrender me... and when Mrs Waddy... addressed me piteously, 'Master Richmond, would you leave papa?' I cried out, 'No, no, never leave my papa', and twisted away from my aunt's keeping. (AHR 4; 44)

Later, abandoned at Dr Rippenger's Academy by this same beloved papa, Harry daydreams, re-entering that phantasmagoric world to which his father belongs. He recites his lessons mechanically whilst in hot mental pursuit of him, faltering as he awakes, disoriented, to the classroom scene around him: 'that made me... ask myself why I was there and he absent' (AHR 5; 51). No one could write more simply and movingly than Meredith once he got into his emotional stride, and the syntactical parallel snaps shut here on an aching sense of loss.

The abrupt shifts of the narrative in these opening chapters are similar to those found at the beginning of *David Copperfield*, leaving a series of loosely connected, almost surreal scenes sharply etched on the mind. This brilliantly evokes the child's consciousness, recalling an earlier note that Meredith sent Charles Kingsley about *Shagpat*, when he talked of 'the mind in a state of childhood, where quick transitions are natural' (*Letters* I: 25). Similar episodes occur later, when sights loom at Harry through fog, smoke and dusk, reaching their apogee when he catches up with his father, momentarily immobilized by his bronze casing, in just such a far-off place as he had imagined as a much younger boy.

But this is later. Whilst still at school, and living 'systematically out of [himself]' (*AHR* 6; 70), Harry's thoughts begin to turn in other directions – to Heriot, the dashing head boy, and the schoolmaster's daughter, Julia Rippenger. His wonder at Heriot's starlit ladder-to-window farewell to Julia, his heaving chest when Heriot departs for military school, the outdoor feast he then holds with money brought by Heriot's aunt, during which the boys' plundered goose is plundered again by tramps – each Wordsworthian 'spot of time' (a phrase Meredith uses himself in *Beauchamp's Career* (*BC* 8; 79)) is captured and held for a moment in all its brilliancy. This is Meredith at his best, and it continues after the disreputable feast is broken up and Harry is sheltered by the gipsy girl Kiomi, before being swept away again and restored to Riversley: 'One minute I was curiously perusing the soft shade of a moustache on my aunt's upper lip; the next, we jumped into the carriage, and she was my dear aunt Dorothy again, and the world began rolling another way' (*AHR* 8; 102). Here, the detail of the moustache is comic, but not just comic. It reveals the hesitation, the one split second between the boy's detached observation of his aunt and his yielding himself up, willy-nilly, to family affection again. But it is clear that Harry's horizon, below the strip of sky that his father once so effectively blocked, is beginning to widen. First at one remove with Julia, then with Kiomi, girls have entered the picture – tempting young girls without the distraction of moustaches.

This is confirmed on the first stage of his adventures in the world beyond school and Riversley, when Harry, now a teenager in physical pursuit of his father, and his friend Temple witness a fire in London. They encounter a pair of jaunty street-walkers and help rescue an old woman in her nightdress, before being 'rescued' themselves by the fanatically religious Captain Welsh. The excitement, confusion – and flames – here suggest that Harry has now indeed entered 'The Magnetic Age' which brought Richard Feverel to his Lucy. This is subsequently confirmed when the boys arrive in Europe, where Harry soon becomes deeply involved in a fairytale romance amid fairytale scenery of silvery firs and crimson sunsets. The object of his affection here is the German princess Ottilia, who herself grows from a charming 12-year-old to a wise, philosophical young woman during the course of the narrative.

His new experiences teach Harry more than he had ever learned from his unstable upbringing in England. Inevitably there comes a time, just before he reaches his majority and receives his inheritance from Squire Beltham, when he is unable to admire his father uncritically: 'The vitality of the delusion I cherished was therefore partly extinct; not so the love; yet the love of him could no longer shake itself free from oppressive shadows' (AHR 22; 258). Through this growing detachment, and a picaresque series of events and involvements in Europe and at home, he does indeed begin to find his own values and identity. By the end of the narrative, both father-figures have died: Squire Beltham a matter of months after another furious showdown with the feckless Richmond, and Richmond himself in fittingly spectacular and fiery fashion, literally going up in smoke on the very last page. Beyond himself now, no longer to be held responsible for his actions, he had been putting on a foolishly ambitious firework display to celebrate the wanderer's return to Riversley, and the old house had caught fire. Harry had by now grown mature enough to pity his father, realizing at last that 'to the rest of the world he was a progressive comedy: and the knowledge made him seem more tragic still. He clearly could not learn from misfortune; he was not to be contained...I chafed at his unteachable spirit, surely one of the most tragical things in life' (AHR 47; 541). These words crystallize much of Meredith's philosophy again, bringing together the call for 'more brain'; the belief that unrealistic self-assessments incur 'thwackings'; and also his continuing faith in an overarching, beneficent power that offers us a 'special governing direction' in our journey through life (*AHR* 15; 178).

There is some redemption for Richmond. Having tried to put out the flames himself, he hurried to the rescue of Harry's aunt Dorothy. It may seem a typically grand and useless gesture, considering that Dorothy, who had loved him, was not even at home. But he was not to know that. Meredith has let him die a hero. Such magnanimity suggests his own recovery from childhood wounds. As for Harry, all he is given to say is that his father 'was never seen again' (*AHR* 56; 685). This is not as offhand as it sounds; we have seen that Meredith writes most simply when most deeply moved. On the other hand, there is undeniably a sense of closure here, of the curtain dropping on a performer whose magic has finally died, and on Harry's childhood too. Riversley, where he had spent the most stable part of it, has gone. The hero's way forward into maturity, into a proper relationship with the larger world which his father had once blotted out, is now clear. And beside him, to help him tackle it, is not his fairytale princess, but his Beltham second-

In a symbolic moment, Harry kisses Janet's hand, while his father, whom she has been looking after, is slumped in an armchair (George du Maurier's illustration to Chapter 50 in *The Cornhill Magazine*, reprinted in the Memorial Edition of the novel (Vol. 10; facing p. 314)).

cousin Janet Ilchester, as solid and English as her name suggests. Once described as someone who 'caught imagination by the sleeve, and shut it between square whitewashed walls' (*AHR* 23; 260), hearty, frowning and tomboyish Janet has blossomed into a beauty all her own, but with her feet still firmly on the ground. She is the perfect person to keep Harry's feet there too.

However memorable they are, it is not so much the big events, the 'great and startling effects' (*Letters* I: 453), that make this novel so significant: Meredith himself said he had meant to steer clear of these. Rather, it is the disclosure of the young hero's unmediated perspective that impresses – that draws readers into his dynamic world, and at the same time leaves them to form their own judgement about what he himself only partially comprehends at each stage of his growth: 'Note, as you read, the gradual changes of the growing Harry, in his manner of regarding his father and the world', wrote Meredith to Hardman in November 1871 (*Letters* I: 453). The mixture of empathy and sympathy thus evoked makes this another powerful reading experience.

4

A New Kind of Hero: From *Beauchamp's Career* to *The Egoist*

Now very much part of the literary establishment, Meredith had been advising Chapman & Hall for over ten years, and had ten books to his credit, including the 1862 volume of poetry containing 'Modern Love', and the two important Bildungsromans. The most recent of these had been serialized in the highly prestigious *Cornhill Magazine*. Yet not even *Harry Richmond*, embarked on as a 'spanking bid for popularity' (*Letters* I: 255), had found widespread favour. Readers not put off by his eccentricities of style and narration still found his plots hard to follow: 'by no means easy reading, if we would understand what is going on, and keep up with the progress of events', wrote A. J. Butler, reviewing *Harry Richmond* in the *Athenaeum* (*CH*, 155). This was not just a question of manner. He still lacked the 'calm command of material' he had once admired in Thackeray (*Letters* 1: 32). Fellow-writer Siegfried Sassoon later put this down to an 'excess of creative excitability'[1] and he was probably right. Now Meredith would finally win over his critics with two well-structured novels exploring, amongst much else, the nature of heroism – *Beauchamp's Career*, which was perhaps his own favourite,[2] and *The Egoist*, for which he is now best known.

BEAUCHAMP'S CAREER

With a return to third-person narration, Meredith had no trouble making Nevil Beauchamp look the part of a hero, a protagonist imbued in his own right with natural dynamism: 'His features, more than handsome to a woman, so mobile they were, shone of sea and spirit, the chance lights of the sea, and the spirit breathing out of it' (*BC* 2; 22). An impetuous lad, a 'hurricane of a youth' (*BC* 10; 87), he is associated throughout with the sea in his vitality, and with fire in his fervour: he is first met trying to challenge a member (any member) of the French Guard to a duel, to defend his country's honour. This is the kind of quixotic 'cloud-work' in which Richard Feverel had indulged; but Meredith gives this latest hero the chance to display his 'knightly manliness' more usefully (*BC* 40; 458). Recent history is better assimilated here than in *Vittoria*: Nevil's uncle and guardian, the Hon. Everard Romfrey, sends him to sea at 14, and the young lieutenant, imbued with the heroic ideals of his favourite 'fire-and-smoke writer', Carlyle, fights so bravely in the Crimea that Romfrey writes to warn him against unnecessary risk-taking (*BC* 2; 23). Equally indicative of the future is what Nevil does once hostilities cease: he dispenses provisions in the

Frederick Maxse, R. N., the original of Nevil Beauchamp, from a contemporary photograph (S. M. Ellis, *George Meredith: His Life and Friends in Relation to His Work* (Grant Richards, 1920, 2nd ed.) facing p.238). Maxse had also fought bravely in the Crimea, and was a great fan of Carlyle's.

French camp. As a result, he catches a fever. To one grateful French officer's father, he is the 'vrai type de tout ce qu'il y a de noble et de chivalresque dans la vieille Angleterre' (*BC* 5; 47–8); but neo-feudalism has segued into a softer-hearted humanitarianism here. Meredith seems not so much 'bent on bringing traditional notions of the "heroic" into question', as on combining them with newer ones.[3] It is as if the dashing Guy of Goshawk and the gentler saviour of Cologne, Farina, have been rolled into one.

Such a hero can be the romantic lead as well as the warrior: Nevil's gallantry now becomes mixed with romance. While he and the young French officer, Roland de Croisnel, are recuperating in Venice, he falls in love with Roland's beautiful sister Renée, and tries to rescue her from the death-in-life of a loveless marriage. She is not yet ready to risk everything for love; like his challenge to the French Guard, the bid is futile. However, his stature is restored along with his health when he volunteers to spy out slavers along the African coast, in order to release their unfortunate cargoes. Lord Romfrey no more approves of this new evidence of Nevil's 'humanitomtity' (*BC* 11; 103), as he mockingly calls it, than of his entanglement with Renée. But Nevil continues to combine older ideas of heroism with newer, kindlier ones, and Romfrey will soon have a worse pill to swallow.

Ignoring his promotion to captain, the moment Nevil lands in England again he abandons his naval career for a political one. To his Whig uncle's renewed disgust, he becomes an ardent disciple of the elderly Dr Shrapnel, an idealistic radical who has been agitating against the Game Law. Taking his own stand as a passionate Radical, Nevil throws himself into the election campaign at nearby Bevisham. Canvassing hard and honestly for votes, he is driven by the longing to make the world a fairer place: 'forgive me for beating my drum', he tells his long-time friend Cecilia Halkett, 'I see what others don't see, or else I feel it more; I don't know; but it appears to me our country needs rousing if it's to live. There's a division between poor and rich that you have no conception of, and it can't be safely left unnoticed.' (*BC* 32; 361) Meredith has evidently joined Nevil on his platform here, allowing himself to come nearer than he ever did elsewhere to the 'Condition of England' novel, not a form of which he generally approved (see *Letters* I: 432); indeed, he worried at the time that he was doing too much of this kind of thing here, especially as he also airs his views on such issues as the country's preparedness for war, and vegetarianism. 'It is philosophical-political', he warned the American author and activist Moncure Conway, describing the work as 'an attempt to show the forces round a young man of the present day, in England, who would move them, and finds them unutterably solid' (*Letters* I: 485). Although Meredith clearly relished using the experience gained by helping Maxse on the campaign trail, and had an eye to the narrative's topical appeal, he decided to cut 'the heavier of the electioneering passages' in preparation for its serialization (*Letters* I: 484). This is one case, therefore, where serialization had a salutary effect on him, making him trim the sails to keep his plot moving.

Nevertheless, we see Nevil's career faltering as his various heroic endeavours pull him in different directions. Still rather quaintly chivalrous, he cannot resist responding to a mysterious summons by Renée, and so loses the election. Also largely as a result of this involvement, he loses Cecilia, who had seemed intended for him from the start (significantly, Maxse's wife's name was Cecilia). A 'splendid prize' worth winning, 'the very woman to nerve and sustain him' (*BC* 23; 239), she accepts his Tory relative Blackburn Tuckham instead. By now, too, Nevil has been seized by his old fixation on honour. Shrapnel, while being deliberately baited, had said something dubious about Rosamund Culling, the widow who runs the Romfrey household and who is soon to become Romfrey's wife. The perceived insult so enraged Nevil's irascible uncle that he had ridden over and horsewhipped the elderly Radical. As a boy, Nevil had fought his cousin over some such innuendo about Rosamund; now it is the affront to his mentor's dignity that upsets him. He cannot rest until his uncle apologizes.

His world disintegrating around him, Nevil again falls ill. He contracts a dangerous fever from visiting someone who had lost his job and been ruined by voting for him.[4] The gesture, he admits later, was not useful. At this juncture all his noble endeavours seem called into question. Jenny Denham, Shrapnel's ward, nurses him through a prolonged delirium in which he talks incessant gibberish.[5]

At last, with the energetic backing of Rosamund herself, the longed-for apology is extracted from Romfrey. It is a small victory, but it is over the high-handed old guard; it marks a turning-point. Another sign of Nevil's revival is his rather unexpected proposal to Jenny. Romfrey sees this in a coolly rational light: 'There's no law against a man marrying his nurse', he says dryly, adding, 'he wants a wife: she accepts a husband. The two women who were in love with him [Renée and Cecilia] he wouldn't have' (*BC* 55; 615). True, the new liaison does not seem to be a passionate one. Nevil's 'work in life' has long since been 'much above the love of a woman in his estimation' (*BC* 24; 248). But the more alert reader may realise that Jenny has been dear to Nevil for some time; Nevil's friend, the Liberal poet and author Lydiard, had noticed her feelings for him, too. And they are well matched. The other women around Nevil fill roles found in earlier novels: Rosamund is rather like Lady Blandish in *Richard Feverel*, and stands in the place of a mother to him; Renée, mysterious and alluring like Princess Ottilia in *Harry Richmond*, is more a distraction than a helpmeet; and Cecilia, too emotionally complex to be called a 'type', nevertheless occupies a similar place in the schematics of the plot to Janet Ilchester's in *Harry Richmond*. But Jenny is different. Not such a 'sister mind' as Nevil supposes (*BC* 56; 623), once their relationship is formalized she asserts herself successfully against his increasing secularism. Here is a new kind of union in which the two must negotiate with each other, and can grow together.

Then, as in *Richard Feverel*, the happy ending already thus instituted is cruelly sabotaged. Putting in to shore after the couple's extended trip to Europe, Nevil tries to save two urchins who have toppled into the river from their father's boat.[6] He drowns, having managed to save one, or perhaps both (the details are blurred here), before going under. Called to the scene, Shrapnel and Romfrey size up the 'insignificant bit of mudbank life' (*BC* 56; 631) fished up by their protégé, and then stare blankly at each other. As the river is dredged on a dark December evening, and onlookers throng around, the two old enemies stand united in a devastating sense of waste. It is one of those unforgettable moments when Meredith's greatness is best seen, when personal history and ideologies drop away and the extremity of human emotion is exposed.

Shrapnel seems to feel here the force of what he had once admitted, in a letter that Romfrey and others had mocked: 'Seeds perish in nature; good men fail' (*BC* 29; 323). Of course, nature has its 'darker way', as Meredith has always acknowledged. But narrative pluralism need not depend on the intrusion of narrators. Meredith has also prepared us for more positive ways of reading this ending. When Renée had unexpectedly turned up in London earlier on, Nevil had had to accept that the situation was beyond him, and that events would have to take their own course. It had been a kind of psychological 'thwacking' for him. At that point, one of Shrapnel's more gnomic pronouncements had been abruptly inserted into the text. For 'the world... to be wrought out', the older man had pronounced, nature has 'to be subdued' (*BC* 42; 481). By this he meant that *our* nature, specifically our wayward tendency to over-estimate our roles in life, must be conquered for the sake of society at large. Nevil had tried to channel the natural force in him, to use it for the better good of others: 'what man of blood fiery as Nevil's ever fought so to subject it?' Rosamund asks herself near the end (*BC* 56; 617). The sacrifice of his life for another is the ultimate in that 'personal abnegation' which Meredith himself saw as the theme of *Beauchamp's Career* (*Letters* I: 484), and the way ahead for the human race.

There is more than a hint here of Darwin's recently published *Descent of Man* (1871), with its discussion of altruistic behaviour in nature, and its contribution to the species.[7] This ties in with the political concerns of the novel: the life Nevil has saved this time with his despised 'humanitomtity' may not seem promising, but from a radical viewpoint, 'the people are the Power to come' (BC 29; 325). This ultimate sacrifice on their behalf confirms both his commitment to their cause, and his fundamental opposition to the self-interested politicking in his background.[8] Besides, he also leaves behind him his son by Jenny, a young woman who is serious, thoughtful, resolute – and motherly. There is every reason to suppose that the fight will be carried forward. In short, with more definite promise than in *Richard Feverel*, the seed has been sown. Such a reading is supported by the author himself, who added in his letter to Conway, 'He does not altogether fail, has not lived quite in vain' (*Letters* 1: 485). Not for the first time, this author has scotched our expectations at the close of the narrative, but not withheld hope.

A note of caution: dwelling exclusively on this last episode distorts the novel. Like all Meredith's work, it blends tragedy with comedy. Fun is poked at practically all the male characters, including the whirligig Nevil and his bigoted and insular uncle, who, for example, views Venice only as a place of mud, mosquitoes and affectation. Then there is Renée's husband, a bald-pated, large-nosed dandy of a marquis; and also a good deal of political satire: Meredith felt that humour had a particularly strong corrective function in this area, serving to chasten those who 'slowed or prevented the democratic operation of politics'.[9] Not even Shrapnel, with whom he seems to have partially identified himself,[10] escapes the caricaturist's pen. As for the women, one of their roles has been to note and convey such comic touches. Lord Palmet's aunt, Mrs Grancey Lespel, is a great tease as well as a gossip, with her witty apercus about men flaunting their uniforms and so on. A wise friend for Cecilia, she knows that the younger woman is strong enough to face the unromantic realities. Another minor character, Reneé's watchful sister-in-law Agnes d'Auffray, serves as a restraining hand on Nevil's shoulder. In general, so illuminating are the more important female protagonists' responses throughout that it is fair to say that 'the novel is written for the most part through a feminine consciousness'.[11] Meredith, as was his wont, would now pick up these aspects of the book – the interrelated roles of comedy and women – in his next novel.

'AN ESSAY ON COMEDY'

First, however, he would link them more consciously in the only public lecture he ever gave: 'On the Idea of Comedy and the Uses of the Comic Spirit', later modified for publication in essay form. Here, showing an easy familiarity with Molière, Restoration comedy, Greek drama, Fielding, Goldsmith, Jane Austen, Cervantes and others, he produced a *tour de force* of synthetical thinking. Never before had comedy and women been given such exalted roles in our culture; his yoking them together still seems unique and highly relevant today.

A man with a memorably hearty laugh, Meredith believed strongly in the healthful power of laughter: the heroine of *Diana of the Crossways* would call it 'the breath of her soul' (*DC* 1; 8). What he had in mind in his lecture was the delight that comes from perceiving discrepancies between what we are, what we think we are, and what we would like to be. Analysing this kind of response and its effects is notoriously difficult, and he manages it partly by looking at other literatures, especially French literature in the age of Molière, and partly by drawing distinctions. The result is simultaneously wide-ranging and dense, with many different examples. But two comments, one on Molière's *Femmes Savantes* and one on Cervante's *Don Quixote*, stand out. The former work, he says, 'is a capital instance in the uses of comedy in teaching the world to understand what ails it' (EC 432); as for the latter,

> The knight's great aims and constant mishaps, his chivalrous valiancy exercised on absurd objects, his good sense along the high road of the craziest of expeditions, the compassion he plucks out of derision, and the admirable figure he preserves while stalking through the frantically grotesque and burlesque assailing him, are in the loftiest moods of humour, fusing the tragic sentiment with the comic narrative. (EC 446)

By the time Meredith gets to Cervantes, the role of the Comic Spirit has been more clearly defined. He has now distinguished it from satire, which he sees as cruel and hurtful, and from irony, which he sees as the agent of satire, capable of stinging, and of being, in its detachment, coldly malicious. He has distinguished it too from the kind of good-natured humour which may involve pity and even, by association, self-pity. These approaches or responses are all either unkind or too kind, distorting the facts. The true Comic Spirit, he believes, is 'the first-born of common sense' (EC 441) – derived literally from a sense of communality – and encourages more gentle but lasting correction. Its role is to reveal to us, as Cervantes does, the human spirit in action as it rises to the many, various and sometimes quite extraordinary challenges of life. The object is not for us to condemn or pity our struggling fellow human-beings, however misguided they might be, but to see where they overstep the mark into pretension and affectation, sentimentalism, or some other absurdity, and so to be set on the right track ourselves. While Meredith fully acknowledges the 'lights of tragedy' in the great humorist's work, he believes that if his constructive spirit prevails there will be 'a bright and positive, clear Hellenic *perception of facts*' (EC 443; emphasis added).

There is an earnestly moral streak in this dissection of the Comic Spirit, something very much of the time. Here is a writer who assumes the fundamental soundness of his society and its values,[12] quite without cynicism – an attitude he abhors, something shown already by Adrian Hartley in *Richard Feverel*, and soon to be confirmed by Sir Willoughby Patterne in *The Egoist*. But his ideas have grown more from his own thinking and practice as a writer than from the cultural context. Indeed, the whole lecture (later published as an essay, and then as a book) can be taken as a determined, public attempt to analyse and justify his preferred *modus operandi* as a novelist. When talking about Don Quixote's 'chivalrous valiancy', he could almost be talking about Shibli Bagarag or the later heroes who suffer 'thwackings' by overreaching themselves, but go on striving and remain attractive to us. The root of all this may lie deep in Meredith's psyche, in his need to boost his own morale but at the same time to accept setbacks; perhaps also in the need for the support and guidance that he himself had lacked in childhood. But whatever the ultimate source, by now this complex of ideas has been integrated into his wider vision, a hopeful vision of life lived in recognition of the 'rights and dues of the world' (EC 448), and in harmony with the whole natural order.

There is another important ingredient in all this. Women have always had a special place in comedy, which traditionally deals with affairs of the heart on a lower level than tragedy, as Meredith himself acknowledges. But in that context, their sharp wits bring them closer to men, even to a 'mutual likeness' (EC 433). Elevating women just as he believes the comedies themselves do, Meredith argues that intelligent women are required in the audience (or readership) as well. The process he describes, of recognition, reflection and response, cannot flourish without a society of cultivated men and women who are 'sufficiently quick-witted and enlightened by education to welcome great works' (EC 431). His example of such a society is the seventeenth-century Parisian bourgeoisie, for whom Molière had written. Where women are excluded, he says, 'you cannot have society, without which the senses are barbarous and the Comic Spirit is driven to the gutters of grossness to slake its thirst' (EC 440). This yoking of women's status not only with a higher function for the Comic Spirit, but also with the general refinement and intellectual receptiveness of society, is *not* very much of the author's time. It is an original and ringing endorsement of John Stuart Mill's quite recently published work, *The Subjection of Women* (1869), which he had read with relish. Positively startling for its age, this assertion reminds us of Meredith's own splendid female protagonists, from Shibli's wise, wonderful and ultimately beautiful Noorna right up to the quartet who constitute the pervasive 'feminine consciousness' of *Beauchamp's Career*.

THE EGOIST

Little wonder, then, that the chief agent of the Comic Spirit in his next novel, *The Egoist*, is the heroine, the brave and resolute Clara Middleton; nor that its target is a supremely egotistical male – the utterly self-centred Sir Willoughby Patterne. But despite being the target, it is still Willoughby who drives forward the plot; and for this very reason the nature of heroism, that is, of what makes a true hero, is still an important issue in the narrative.

Brought up like a little prince, doted on by his widowed mother and unmarried aunts, admired by all around him, Willoughby certainly seems like the kingpin. He has one central motive: to bolster his position with a wife who will make him the envy of his world, and who will perpetuate his line with healthy stock. Love hardly comes into it; he seems incapable of feeling it. Even so, his goal eludes him. Quite unaccountably (that is to say, *he* cannot account for it), he is jilted by his first choice, the beautiful, well-to-do, ironically named Constantia Durham. In fact, both Constantia and the reader are alerted to Willoughby's true nature when he snubs a relative, Lieutenant Crossjay Patterne, simply because the marine's unprepossessing figure falls short of his reputation for heroism. Characteristically enough, Willoughby has confused appearance with reality. Shrugging off his humiliating treatment by Constantia, Willoughby first dallies with the adoring but unportioned and delicate Laetitia Dale, daughter of a tenant on his estate, then cruelly abandons her. Instead, he sweeps another, more suitable candidate off her feet in a 'whirlwind wooing' (*E* 5; 34). This is Clara Middleton. She is only 18, but he refuses to give her time to consider his proposal properly, or to gain more experience of the world, and pressures her into plighting her troth formally. Unwilling to risk another debacle, he wants to secure her even before marriage. But, having failed to understand why his earlier fiancée decamped, he quickly displays his superficial, self-centred and possessive behaviour all over again. What he wants, he tells Clara, is nothing less than to be 'the possessor of the whole of you. Your thoughts, hopes, all!' (*E* 9; 71). We share her revulsion as his character unfolds for her, deftly revealed as destructive, essentially anti-life and of course completely unheroic. Clara gets to hear about his treatment of the marine as well; another clue for her (and us) is his refusal to re-employ the ex-coachman Flitch, a poor man with a huge family, who had left in order to try, unsuccessfully as it turned out, to better himself. 'I am unforgiving when I have been offended', Willoughby announces smugly (*E* 9; 72). Worse, Willoughby threatens to treat his equable cousin Vernon Whitford, now managing his estates, in exactly the same way should he ever leave Patterne Hall. Even Colonel Horace de Craye, a guest at the Hall, recognizes this 'stiff, strange, exacting' vein in Willoughby (*E* 22; 178).

Meredith makes us aware that heredity and circumstances had both conspired to make Clara susceptible to Willoughby's charms at first: her mother had been an impulsive 'firework' of a woman (*E* 22; 156), and her widowed father, a scholarly cleric absorbed in his Latin cruxes, had been eager for his daughter to make a good marriage. However, it is now established as a mismatch, with Clara emerging as the chief yardstick against which Willoughby is to be judged. She is all that he is not. Whereas he is cynical, only loves himself, and is actually proud of being 'insensible to change' (*E* 31; 257), Clara loves life and is responsive to change, enjoying the alternation of the seasons with a 'watchful happiness', and embracing and sympathizing with the whole panoply of rural life, from wild flowers to the poor cottagers. She includes in her delight the poetry and books which touch her heart: 'She dwelt strongly on that sincerity of feeling; it gave her root in our earth' and filled her with 'joyful optimism' (E 19; 149–50). Meredith's whole poetic feel for life, its expression in verse set aside for now because of the premium on bread-winning, is freshly and succinctly embodied in her.

Willoughby had assumed that Clara was drawn to him instinctively, as the fittest mate for her, but he was miserably wrong. Her own nature being what it is, she gravitates towards his unostentatious, impecunious but more generous and vital cousin instead. She discovers that Vernon has taken on himself the charge of Lieutenant Crossjay's eldest son, and that Willoughby only plays at being the lad's benefactor, spoiling him and currying favour with him. Vernon on the other hand is trying conscientiously to prepare the 12-year-old for the naval career he has set his heart on. Here we are being introduced to another kind of hero, then, a much better kind. Clara and Vernon are united in their affection for young Crossjay, a good-hearted lad whose role is like one of the mischievous, watchful, revealing imps whom Meredith describes early in the novel as 'the dogs and pets of the Comic Spirit' (E 2; 10). Clara races him, Vernon chases him to bring him to his lessons, and the pair are often in motion around him amid the beautiful natural surroundings of the Hall. Mrs Mountstuart Jenkinson, one of the more acerbic and pithy of Meredith's wise older women,[13] points out early on that Willoughby 'has a leg' (E 2; 12); but this only suggests his striking a pose:[14] he had engaged in sport simply to excel, and finds even walking 'a sour business' (E 4; 26). Clara, Vernon and Crossjay, on the other hand, are active, energetic and truly alive in the present, revelling in activity for its own sake. They tire themselves in a healthy fashion, not from mere *ennui*. Vernon, for example, is so much at one with nature that he falls asleep under the wild cherry-tree, with its gloriously rich but short-lived double blossoms signifying the fullness and beauty of the moment. Coming upon him there, Clara feels that he 'must be good who loves to lie and sleep beneath the branches of this tree' (E 11; 95). Later, when she watches Vernon and Crossjay going to bathe in the lake, she sees the pair merging into the elements: '[t]hey seemed to Clara made of morning air and clear lake-water' (*E* 21; 170–1). Their responsiveness to nature is the route to *joie de vivre*, and Laetitia is at pains to explain to Clara that although Vernon is anxious at this time, normally 'there is no laugh like Vernon Whitford's, and no humour like his' (*E* 32; 267). Amongst the other virtues attributed to this alternative hero are his devotion as a friend and his tireless walking, confirming that he was based on Meredith's fellow 'Sunday Tramp' Leslie Stephen (see *SL*, 193n.) and indicative of his having something of his author in him too.

Hand in hand with Vernon's energy goes a vital inner life. To some extent, Willoughby expresses the showy, bluff outer man, while Vernon represents the sensitive self within. The former is displayed to advantage in company; the latter is not: Vernon is such a hopeless dance-partner that he provokes laughter, and invites comparisons to 'Theseus in the maze', or 'a fly released from a jam-pot' or even, most tellingly, 'a "salvage" [wild], or green, man caught in a web of nymphs and made to go the paces' (*E* 3; 15). Such was the contrast when Willoughby took him to America on his three-year grand tour after the original jilting, that Vernon seemed his foil, 'a new kind of thing, nondescript, produced in England of late, and not likely to come to much good himself, or do much good to the country' (*E* 4; 23). Indeed, in contrast to the titled landowner just setting out on his life, Vernon was already a scholar and, we learn later, an unfortunate widower. Even now, he lacks not only bearing and money, but status as well. He himself feels that he is 'no hero' (*E* 27; 222). Yet even on the occasion when he says this, we can see his true worth. Willoughby, determined to avoid being jilted a second time, has kept Clara's father at the Hall by plying him with vintage port. Guided initially by young Crossjay, Clara has therefore struck out on her own. Vernon has caught up with her, drenched from a storm, at the railway station. Instead of pressuring her as Willoughby had done, he now attends to her shelter, comfort and moral welfare, putting the facts to her plainly and simply, and reminding her of the effects her actions will have on others. Astutely, he protects her reputation by distracting Mrs Mountstuart when her carriage draws up at the station. Clara responds. She is steadied and righted: 'Vernon's wish that she should have her free will, compelled her to sound it: and it was of course to go, to be liberated, to cast off incubus:

– and hurt her father? Injure Crossjay? distress her friends? No, and ten times no!' (*E* 27; 224) His delicate handling of the situation, and his good sense, impress Clara as well as the reader: she returns to Patterne Hall.

Meanwhile, the puncturing of inflated Willoughby, and of any lurking feeling we might have for him, continues apace. Meredith's previous egoists have either begun to search their hearts and listen to nature (or to sound advice from a woman, much the same thing with this author); or else, like Sir Austin Feverel and Roy Richmond, they have become to some degree pitiable. His latest egoist, the strutting General Ople in the short story, 'The Case of General Ople and Lady Camper', became pitiable quite soon: he received such a barrage of revealing caricatures from his widowed neighbour that it almost sent him mad before curing him. But Willoughby neither learns nor is pitiable. In order to make out that the change of heart is his, not Clara's, he quickly proposes to Laetitia. However, Laetitia is no longer the amenable companion of his youth: she writes poetry, and is intelligent and perceptive; her adoration has failed to survive his callous treatment of her. She has changed much more realistically than, and in an opposite way to, Noorna in *The Shaving of Shagpat*. To Willoughby's amazement and horror, she rejects him, leaving him to hurry back to Clara again and act the part of a desperate lover. And he *is* desperate, in a way. So panic-stricken is he now at the prospect of being *thrice*-jilted, and a laughing-stock, that neither woman's happiness is of any account to him. At this juncture he stands fully revealed to us not as the hero he had thought himself, but as a monster of deception as well as self-deception, his artificially impassioned declarations to *both* women contrasting dramatically with the 'stone-man' within (*E* 10; 82).

The confusion that ensues is quite astounding, with almost the whole cast assembling at Patterne Hall, and nobody knowing who is about to be married to whom, least of all the principals themselves.[15] Misunderstandings arise not only from Willoughby's bewildering about-turns but also from various types of failures of communication. Some are purely farcical, such as Laetitia's mistaking Willoughby's knock at her door for Clara's, and issuing a welcome which Willoughby tries to capitalize on. Others arise from the language itself. We cannot help noticing that those on the side of nature speak from their hearts: words tumble and burst out of Crossjay, any holding back costs him acute discomfort. As for the rest, words obfuscate rather than reveal. For example, neither Dr Middleton nor Willoughby can communicate with Laetitia's father, Dr Dale, a gentle invalid alarmed by his daughter's recent distress. Dr Middleton is convinced that Willoughby has only proposed to her on Vernon's behalf, but uses such incomprehensible words and circumlocutions that the invalid confesses that his head is spinning. 'For facts, we are bradypeptics to a man, sir', agrees Dr Middleton pleasantly (*E* 44; 378), meaning only that we all find it hard to digest facts, but leaving Dr Dale more mystified than ever. For his part, Willoughby, being still uncertain of the outcome himself, deliberately avoids explaining what has happened: 'There are situations, Mr Dale, too delicate to be clothed in positive definitions' (*E* 46; 394).

The misuse of language here is comic enough, but upsetting for Mr Dale, and in that respect useful for the resolution of the plot; Laetitia has to be fetched to minister to him. She cannot refuse to answer such a summons; nor, in the end, can she refuse Willoughby. Even Clara, softening towards her ex-fiancé once she is free of him, urges him on her: 'Could you resist him, so earnest as he is?' (*E* 49; 418), she pleads. But Laetitia takes Willoughby on with eyes wide open to his defects, and from this point on, order begins to be restored. Assuming from Clara the corrective function of the Comic Spirit, Laetitia shocks his aunts by announcing in their presence that she is marrying without love, and demands in front of them that young Crossjay should be properly educated and welcomed in their home, and Flitch given another chance. It is the first of what promises to be a lifetime of 'lashings' (*E* 49; 421) for Willoughby. But he is in too tight a corner, and too distracted by the sight of Mrs Mountstuart's carriage approaching outside, to bother about any future programme. He is only alarmed in case his new guest draws an unfavourable contrast between the blooming bride he has lost and the faded one he is getting. Any sympathy we might be tempted to feel for him here is thus forfeited, even though Laetitia has none of the qualifications of 'money...health and beauty' expected of a Patterne bride (*E* 3; 15). Instead, we take pleasure in his deflation, and especially in knowing that Laetitia plans to distribute the Patterne wealth to good causes, and travel abroad to lands she has only imagined. Willoughby, who hugs everything to himself and likes to play the feudal lord at Patterne Hall and 'shut out the world' (*E* 9; 71), will obviously pay heavily for gaining her.[16] He can only comfort himself now by saying that he has the 'lady with brains!' The narrator adds pointedly, and with a flourish that neatly turns Willoughby into the archetypal henpecked husband, 'He had: and he was to learn the nature of that possession in the woman who is our wife' (*E* 49; 422).

While the balance of power changes so dramatically for these two, it changes between Willoughby and Vernon as well. Willoughby thinks he is in charge when he consigns Clara to Vernon. Blinded by the idea that he himself is the best match for her, he has no idea that the pair are already in love. He simply wants to spite Colonel de Craye, someone of his own kind, with whom he has a history of rivalry and whom he suspects of being his rival now. But of course, as we realized long ago, it is Vernon whom Clara loves, and Vernon (again) who really knows how to handle the situation. He does so with his usual tact and restraint. Being 'practised in self-mastery', he lets Clara signify her own feelings before acknowledging his: 'she loved him the more' for it (*E* 48; 415). Willoughby's concern for his own reputation, his total insensitivity to others, and his sheer vindictiveness, have simply allowed this 'new kind' of hero to supplant him.

*

Three closely entwined threads of imagery contribute to the 'proper degree of roundness and finish' which the author himself appreciated in *The Egoist* (*SL*, 197). First, the clever echo of the willow pattern in Willoughby's name links him with the legend of the jilted lover behind that popular design of china (see Norton, 453–60). Then, Mrs Mountstuart's reference to Clara as 'a dainty rogue in porcelain' gives an early hint of the troubles in store from that quarter for Willoughby (*E* 5; 37). Later, the shattering of wedding-present china, a vase from Colonel de Craye no less, indicates the nature of that trouble even if it is misleading as to the gentleman concerned. That a drunken Flitch is responsible for the breakage, but that as a result Clara is saved from injury, is obviously highly appropriate too. Finally, a china tea service that arrives intact from Lady Busshe puts further pressure on Clara to make the bid for freedom which Vernon intercepts: 'And wedding-presents! and congratulations! And to be his guest!' she tells Vernon in despair after its arrival (*E* 27; 225).

It is tempting to dismiss all this china imagery as largely 'artifice for artifice's sake' as Robert D. Mayo assumes it to be (Norton, 460), especially since Oscar Wilde later made fine china the very mark of aestheticism. But apart from the incidental aptness of each strand, there is an important general point here. This highly civilized society of ours is in reality so fragile, so purely ornamental, and so much under stress from our true nature and our deepest needs, that it will give way, Meredith feels, at some point. This is not necessarily a disaster. It leads to variations, adjustments, assimilations. In the true scientific spirit, it can lead to a fuller life.[17]

And that is just what has happened here. Evolution involves moving forward beyond the self, being open to change. Meredith's own particular view through 'Mr. Darwin's glasses', as he puts it in 'The House on the Beach' (5; 40), and his own class sympathies, [18] encouraged him to see the Whitfords of this world as more likely to thrive than the snobbish self-enclosed Patternes. Like Crossjay's father, they may not look like heroes, but they are. Meredith has rewarded his heroine for her pluck by matching her with one of these instead of with Willoughby. He also spared a thought for Laetitia: she may have missed out on the romance for which she had longed, yet stands to gain much from her new position. By a readjustment of our expectations of the heroic, the author has cleverly produced the best possible conclusion from all the high comedy of the last chapters.

5

The Later Novels: Meredith as Feminist?

As *The Egoist* shows, Meredith's most important women characters have become too complex to undergo fairytale metamorphoses, or even (as Clara's softening towards Willoughby and Laetitia's stunning honesty in front of his aunts illustrates) to toe their author's own anti-sentimentalist, anti-sensationalist line. In his last few novels, Meredith creates another tranche of heroines who respond like flesh and blood to their predicaments. To be sure, even when matched with the less dominant sort of hero, they never gain complete independence. But this was not because Meredith was, after all, 'one of the boys'.[1] Rather, it was because of his abiding concern with the larger purposes of nature.

'THE TALE OF CHLOE' AND *THE TRAGIC COMEDIANS*

Admittedly, not all his later heroines are inspirational. 'The Tale of Chloe', a novella from the same year as *The Egoist*, and *The Tragic Comedians*, a full-length novel from the following year (1880), illustrate the poles between which his views of women have swung. Although both heroines are intriguing in different ways, neither, as he himself seems to have recognized, offers a viable way forward for women readers.

Chloe is introduced as pure-hearted but with a 'playfellow air', a 'frolic spirit' that distinguishes her from the usual angelic archetype beloved of the Victorians (Chloe 5; 233). Living in Regency Bath, she has given her heart and fortune to the faithless Sir Martin Caseldy, who now plans to elope with the young but already married duchess whom Chloe is chaperoning. As the duchess creeps out of their lodging house, she encounters an obstacle. For a moment she is 'ready to laugh, ready to shriek' at the strange hindrance (Chloe 10; 263), but then she realizes (horror!) that the object is a body. The virtuous Chloe has hanged herself from the door, giving up her own life to prevent the younger woman's ruin and its possible consequences. The duchess's screams bring Caseldy himself running in, and such is the confusion both outside and inside the house that the narrator here, Beau Beamish, half-smiling in incredulity, asks the landlady which of the two women within has died. Chloe's idea was that her foolish protégé and the unworthy Caseldy would both be spared the repercussions of their folly; chastened by her death, they would then go on to live better lives. But the near-hysteria of these scenes detracts from any serious appreciation of her dramatic gesture. It neither touches us like Nevil Beauchamp's spur-of-the-moment self-sacrifice, nor carries the symbolic weight of his heroism.

The comic 'lights' of Meredith's next novel, *The Tragic Comedians*, are equally disconcerting, and do even less to offset its sensationalism. Here, the two main characters are 'real creatures' (*TC* preface; 2). Alvan and Clotilde are based, respectively, on the German-Jewish political activist Ferdinand Lasalle and the woman he loved, the blue-blooded Hélène von Dönniges. Their true-life story had ended in 1864 with Lasalle dying in a duel over Hélène, who then promptly married his opponent. Meredith borrows the outline of this bizarre case, but freights it with an assortment of richly suggestive imagery from history, literature and myth,[2] and, of course, with his own vision. It is Alvan, not Clotilde, who dominates the narrative. He is a Hercules, a Titan, a hero after this author's own heart, the sort of larger-than-life character that Meredith loved to draw, and one endowed with just that feeling for the brotherhood of man that he always admired. Yet there is another side to him. This other side is not simply hinted at, as in the case of the 'Chief' in *Vittoria*, who also has his detractors; it is plainly exposed. For all his noble qualities, Alvan is as great and self-destructive an egoist as Willoughby. His supreme self-confidence makes him feel he can just 'brush away' all obstacles in his path (*TC* 5; 53): 'do you suppose me likely to be beaten?' he asks at one point, tempting the ministrations of the Comic imps

(*TC* 10; 118). That being the case, is Clotilde a scourge or a victim? The answer must be 'neither'. She is certainly not a victim. Despite the echoes in her name, she is unlike either Clara Middleton or Chloe. She *wishes* to be mastered, and is driven also by a desire to escape the parental roof. As a result, she actively puts herself in Alvan's way and exercises her feminine wiles on him. Later, her golden locks remind him of serpents, recalling the suspected wife of 'Modern Love'. It is the less surprising, then, that in a fairly pragmatic response to her changed situation, she should turn to the unexpected victor of the duel, young Prince Marko. At this point, an altruistic motive is assigned to her, that she might make Marko happy or at least nurse him till he dies. But it rings hollow, and comes too late to marshal our sympathies.[3]

Sassoon admits to having 'needed an evening with *Cranford* or *Emma* to restore [his] serenity' after rereading *The Tragic Comedians*.[4] His examples are significant: Meredith was often not simply too difficult but too *different* to be appreciated.

DIANA OF THE CROSSWAYS

Only by taking up a home-grown *cause célèbre*, in this case the story of Lady Caroline Norton's acrimonious marriage-breakdown, and creating a heroine with whom both he and his readers could identify, could Meredith at last win over the public, and say what he really wanted to say about women.

Even now, in 1885, readers had to take him as they found him. Subtitled 'On Diaries and Diarists', the opening chapter of *Diana of the Crossways* is a metafictional romp as complex as anything that preceded it, introducing the eponymous heroine through diary entries and memoirs, and commentaries on them. Diana had, it seems, impressed many with her beauty and intelligence, and been remembered for all her pithy and droll sayings. From the start, Meredith puts much of himself into her, giving her some of his own problems as a novelist, and implicating a large age-gap in the failure of her first marriage.[5] The accounts 'quoted' here are generous, making us anticipate meeting Diana for ourselves; but some, apparently, have been less sympathetic, metaphorically digging up the grave and transforming 'the quiet worms, busy on a single poor peaceable body, into winged serpents' (*DC* 1; 9). How then are we to approach Diana's story? With Philosophy, argues the narrator – a balance of heart and brain. Only thus 'fortified', he says, can we see a life as 'humanly shapely', with its 'internal history' making it truly comprehensible. Meredith's discourse on how to read a life thus evolves into a vindication of thoroughgoing psychological probing. 'Wherewith let us to our story, the froth being out of the bottle', the narrator concludes (*DC* 1; 15–20). But of course, as with the opening diatribe about politics in *Beauchamp's Career*, the points made here are not forgotten. They establish the parameters of the narrative, with Meredith showing the springs of his heroine's actions and decisions as her story moves forward to its resolution, and inviting us to 'read' or interpret them intelligently.

Fortunately for the reader, the story itself is firmly grounded in time and place. Meredith had met Caroline Norton during the early days of his first marriage, because she was a close friend of Lady Duff Gordon.[6] She was middle-aged then, and had already passed through the worst of the traumas attendant on her wretched marriage. But Diana, her fictional representative, is first seen much earlier, in her youthful bloom. This places her at a time when men might still duel over a woman's good name, as Mr Sullivan Smith itches to do in Chapter 3; a time, too, when a man expected as his prize 'a still woman, who can make a constant society of her pins and needles' – Diana's own words, as recalled in the first chapter (*DC* 1; 13). Attractive and vivacious, Diana is nevertheless vulnerable. Her parents are dead, her beloved childhood home, Crossways, tenanted by the Warwicks. She marries their nephew Augustus Warwick largely to escape unwanted attentions from others, including those of her close friend Emma's husband, Sir Lukin Dunstane; and also because she longs to be restored to Crossways. But, much as in real life George Norton had sued Lord Melbourne for adultery with his wife, Warwick suspects her of indiscretions with the elderly Lord Dannisburgh. Even though his suit fails, as George Norton's had done, Diana's name is tarnished. This would all have resonated deeply with readers, who had also snapped up Trollope's *He Knew He was Right*, which echoed the Norton story in 1869 when both Caroline Norton and her manipulative husband were still alive.[7]

If topicality added to the heroine's impact when the novel first came out, the setting enhances her even now. Crossways Farm still stands at its crossroads, albeit in Surrey rather than by the Sussex Downs.[8] But, as usual in Meredith's work, the local countryside is much more than a backdrop to her dilemmas. Chapter 19, for example, headed 'A Drive in Sunlight and a Drive in Moonlight', is very much a chapter of light and shade. Diana has recently returned from the Mediterranean, and is riding with Emma through the well-wooded scenery that Meredith himself so loved:

> Through an old gravel-cutting a gateway led to the turf of the down... the dark ridge of the fir and heath country ran companionably to the South-west... Yews, junipers, radiant beeches, and gleams of the service-tree or the white-beam spotted the semicircle of swelling green Down black and silver. The sun in the valley sharpened his beams on squares of buttercups, and made a pond a diamond.

Crossways Farm, noted for its rural charm, as sketched by Hugh Thomson for Eric Parker's *Highways and Byways in Surrey* (Macmillan, 1921), 321. Its name suggests Diana's difficult choices, including that between rootedness and freedom.

Diana is so taken with the dappled view that she cries, 'I should like to build a hut on this point, and wait for such a day to return. It brings me to life' (*DC* 19; 213). But the moment of typically Meredithian exhilaration is followed immediately by bad news. Lord Dannisburgh has died in town. Risking her reputation still further, Diana decides to go and watch by his body that night, and is increasingly enveloped in the 'dark' overtones of the plot. Examining Meredith's claims to eminence in 1886, a year after *Diana* was published, W. L. Courteney, editor of the *Daily Telegraph* and the *Fortnightly*, wrote of 'the true artistic feeling with which Mr Meredith places his characters in an atmospheric background of nature' (*CH*, 289).

As Diana is persecuted for her independent spirit, Meredith again reveals the kind of understanding and compassion that he had shown for such earlier female protagonists as the 'fallen' Dahlia Fleming, the entrapped Clara Middleton, the toyed-with Laetitia Dale, and the betrayed Chloe. But there is a difference, especially from the too-perfect Chloe. Wronged as she is, Diana also *does* wrong, not naively or out of love, but because she is in debt. Having left her husband and successfully established herself as a novelist and socialite in town, she has lost money in an investment and run up bills by living in style and holding dinner parties attended by Lord Dannisburgh's nephew, the MP Percy Dacier. Her beloved Crossways has had to be put up for sale. Impelled almost by a force beyond herself, in a kind of 'swoon of the mind' (Meredith's explanation to a younger friend puzzled by this episode, *Letters* III: 1452) she leaks to the press Dacier's important advance information about the repeal of the Corn Laws. Dacier, with whom she had once almost eloped, is shocked, and hastily retreats to the prim, bloodless young heiress with whom he had had a previous understanding. Realizing now the enormity of what she has done, Diana herself is even more deeply shocked. Fast on the heels of this comes news of Warwick's death in a carriage accident; ironically, she would now have been free to marry Dacier herself. It is all too much for her, and her collapse at this point is plausible. So too is her recovery, helped first by loving, sensible, supportive Emma – and then by nature. Burning the cheque from the newspaper, she allows herself to be taken to her friend's Surrey home to recuperate. Gradually, among the beautiful surroundings, her spirit and her deeper feelings start to revive.

The heading for Chapter 39, in which Diana has to greet Dacier with his new wife, includes the words, 'a short excursion in anti-climax'. Never one for longueurs, Meredith lifts the narrative again by sending two admirers, a young poet called Arthur Rhodes and the utterly solid and loyal Thomas Redworth, to join her in the countryside. The latter had wanted to propose to her long ago, when he was too poor to do so, and has recently bought up Crossways in the hope of restoring her to her home. His role is beginning to fall into place: it was he who had prevented the duel at the beginning; he who had stopped her fleeing abroad when her husband brought his suit against her; and he who had unwittingly forestalled her elopement with Dacier. 'I am always at crossways, and he rescues me', says Diana (*DC* 27; 308). Wealthy by now as a result of railway investments, Redworth is nevertheless still in touch with nature. Meredith is clearly guiding him into the role of the new hero, though one less inclined to nap under cherry blossoms than Vernon Whitford. As his name suggests, he has some fire about him.[9] Slowly, slowly, and with a great deal of edgy resistance from Diana herself and encouragement from Emma, the heroine's feelings are rekindled. Another – the final – chapter heading sums it up: the 'barely willing woman [is] led to bloom with the nuptial sentiment'.

So there it is, taking us somewhat by surprise: the least ambiguously happy ending since *Evan Harrington*. Or is it? There is, in fact, no 'failure of critical reflection' here.[10] On the contrary, Meredith shows Diana herself worrying in case Crossways has been 'turned into a trap' for her (*DC* 40; 451), and feeling a loss of autonomy, a sense of sailing back into harbour, a 'derelict, bearing a story of the sea; empty of ideas' (*DC* 43; 488). In this way, he fully acknowledges some disappointment: despite her brave spell of writing and hostessing in London, Diana is not one of those 'valiant few' to which she herself had once referred, women who escape domesticity to 'form a vanguard' (*DC* 1; 14). Unlike such remarkable figures in earlier Victorian novels as Lucy Snowe in Charlotte Brontë's *Villette* (1853), or Gwendolen Harleth in George Eliot's *Daniel Deronda* (1874), Meredith's best-known heroine takes the conventional route, treading again the well-worn path to the altar.

Yet 'Philosophy', discerning what is 'humanly shapely' in a life, provides a more positive perspective. Entrapment is not an issue in a relationship like Diana's and Redworth's; and there are larger purposes to be served by their marriage. Caroline Norton had had children before her divorce, and her greatest spur to action had been her desire for access to them. Meredith, however, has saved maternity for Diana's future. Showing her lifting up and kissing a small child outside her cottage porch when leaving for the wedding, he demonstrates her readiness to play her part in the all-important evolutionary process. And she will do so, he suggests, sooner rather than later: her fingers give an 'involuntary little twitch' (*DC* 43; 494) when Emma expresses her hope of becoming a godmother to her infant.[11]

No one knew better than Meredith that marriage is a beginning, not an ending, and that it can fall horribly short of expectations. Diana's previous experience of it had been nightmarish, and Emma's marriage has hardly been ideal either, as Sir Lukin had remorsefully acknowledged when his wife was undergoing surgery. Nevertheless, weighing the pros and cons with the author, most readers may conclude that Diana has finally made the right choice.

THE LAST NOVELS

Still exploring ways of living more fully, in greater harmony with each other and nature, Meredith presents us with not just one but several 'Amazing Marriages' in his last three completed novels. Working on this 'obsessive theme',[12] he creates women characters who become progressively stronger in dealing with difficult relationships.

As its title suggests, *One of Our Conquerors*, the earliest of these novels, focuses primarily on the hero. Nevertheless, it features two of Meredith's most endearing heroines. The first is Nataly, whose 'marriage' to Victor Radnor, the 'conqueror' of the title, is amazing because it has never taken place. Victor's legally wedded wife, a much older woman whom he had married in his youth, has steadfastly refused to divorce him. But the young couple had set up home together anyway, and have continued thus for about twenty years now. Nevil Beauchamp's anti-clericalism is a fair reflection of Meredith's at this stage of his life, so no word of blame is uttered here. On the contrary, thinking back, Nataly is allowed to see her surrender to Victor in lyrically natural terms. It was like 'the detachment of a flower on the river's bank by swell of flood', she recalls, adding, 'she had no longer root of her own'. This view is entirely in keeping with her gentle personality. If it was a kind of madness for a woman of her times, well then, says the narrator, 'Love is a madness, having heaven's wisdom in it – a spark. But even when it is driving us on the breakers, call it love: and be not unworthy of it, hold to it'. She is, indeed, still in love with Victor, who is like a 'breath of life' to her (OC 6; 51). She must trust him, believe in him, or fall into despair.

Yet we are soon shown that her trust is misplaced. For Victor, rich financier that he is, and as generously endowed with life as with money, is not one of Meredith's new breed of heroes, but another of his egoists. His current project is to build a grand estate in the Surrey countryside, set in extensive grounds where nature will be bent to his will – tall pines will frame the house, asparagus beds will supply the table, and so on. All this is a trial to Nataly. We learn that she has already had to leave much-loved homes as rumours followed them, and that, as Victor too knows full well, all she wants is 'a secluded modest cottage' where she can shield their daughter Nesta from the taint of illegitimacy – especially now that the girl is of marriageable age (OC 6; 49). But he goes on with the ostentatious 'Lakelands', engaging in his own very concrete version of Richard Feverel's 'cloudwork'. We see what Victor fails to see, that Nataly is becoming positively ill with the worry of it. We cannot share his shock when she dies – ironically enough, just before the long-awaited death of his elderly wife, which would have allowed them to legitimize their union at last.

We do, however, share his sorrow. Although Nataly's role is overshadowed by Victor's here, she is by no means a weak character. On the contrary, in one important way she is stronger than her common-law husband. She is the one with 'more brain'. Victor has all along been trying to catch hold of some great but dimly-perceived 'Idea' that came to him in the memorable opening scene, when he slipped on London Bridge. The working-class man who helped him to his feet on that occasion had accidentally sullied his pristine white waistcoat. Victor's annoyance had provoked the Good Samaritan, in return, to criticize his 'dam punctilio' (*OC* 1; 3). Ruffled by this retort, Victor had pondered his attitude to 'the mob', in the process unconsciously unmasking his class and other prejudices.[13] The bump he received on the back of his head, and his wandering thoughts, continued to bother him. Only Nataly was able to understand why. A beacon of courage beside the stumbling Victor, she helped him see how he has really slipped up in life, and what has really sullied him. She, who thought in terms of nature, was the one to show him what was wrong with his values. He has indeed been too concerned with his image, too pretentious; he has not obeyed Nature's law in his public life as in his private life. Grasping at least 'the skirts of his Idea', Victor had accepted from her a new vision, that 'we the wealthy will not exist to pamper flesh' but 'for the promotion of brotherhood'. England, he at last perceived, 'must make some great moral stand, if she is not to fall to the rear and down' (*OC* 40; 485). He still could not formulate his thoughts well. These preachy words hardly expressed the revelation which he had sensed to be 'surpassingly luminous, alive, a creation' (*OC* 40; 479). But they were the best he could manage before Nataly was suddenly removed from him.

This event, which he had been too preoccupied to foresee, calls him away from the House of Commons on the verge of delivering what promised to be a highly radical speech. As so often, a key event in Meredith's narrative is therefore circumvented; we are left to imagine what he might have said. From now on Victor is a broken man, so deranged by his loss that he has to spend the rest of his foreshortened life in an institution. His incoherent mutterings are like Nevil Beauchamp's during his fever, but for him there is no recovery. Despite having been perhaps Meredith's most appealing egoist, with a heart to be broken, Victor is also perhaps the most harshly treated.

Nesta, however, emerges from her parents' tragedies unscathed. Like the Harrington children in *Evan Harrington*, she has something of each of them in her. Fortunately, what she inherits is the best of both. She is perceptive, sensitive and in tune with nature like her mother, and forthright and active in society like her father. Even before realizing the two were unmarried, she shows soundness of heart and strength of will by staunchly befriending 'Mrs Marsett', a woman in a similar situation to her mother's. There was no need, it seems, to protect her so carefully from the truth about her background. She accepts it; and the loss of one conventionally-minded suitor only facilitates her union with another of a different stamp. More positive about marriage than Diana Warwick/Redworth, she finds a true 'ally' in Dartrey Fenellan, 'whom she owned for leader, her fellow soldier, warrior friend, hero, of her own heart's mould, but a greater' (*OC* 42; 511). The juxtapositions here are sure to raise some hackles; they betray the old need in Meredith of someone to look up to. But it is clear that Nesta will not be as dependent on the man in her life as her mother was. She has her own agenda, to teach others besides Mrs Marsett 'what is actually meant by the good living of a shapely life' (*OC* 42; 513). She herself fully vindicates her parents' union. As her father's cousins had noted, 'The concrete presence of dear Nesta silenced and overcame objections to her being upon earth' (*OC* 24; 296).

Meredith's willingness to make a common-law marriage central to the novel is no surprise. He had shown his sympathy for women in such positions long ago in *Richard Feverel*, and again in *Rhoda Fleming*. More striking here is his greater inwardness in describing such women's feelings, and the repercussions for whoever else is involved. The interior monologues in *One of Our Conquerors* presage the stream-of-consciousness technique of the next generation of writers, and convey a painful sense of the elusiveness of words, and their inadequacy to express what is really meant.[14] The novel thus demonstrates, in a very postmodern way, not only the gaps between what we are and what we seem, but the gap between what we think and what we say. It also reveals the profound psychic cost for an individual like Victor in living out of tune with nature.

*

Shorter, less complex and profound, *Lord Ormont and His Aminta* examines not one but two questionable 'marriages', and again opens the way for one based on true feeling. The first marriage, between the title characters, is of doubtful legitimacy. Aminta meets the 60-year-old Ormont, an unfairly discredited hero of the Indian Mutiny, while on a voyage to Spain with her aunt. She marries him in a ceremony at the British Embassy in Madrid, but, as Ormont's disapproving sister Lady Charlotte points out, 'the name was not published' (*LO* 2; 36). Indeed, Lady Charlotte later claims to have 'positive proof' that the ceremony was a sham (*LO* 13; 164). Perhaps this uncertainty makes it a little easier for Aminta to leave Ormont for his erstwhile secretary and her own admirer from schooldays, Matthew Weyburn, aptly nicknamed 'Matey'. Perhaps it was also meant to help readers accept their action. At any rate, for seven years, these two have the same kind of 'amazing marriage' as Victor Radnor and Nataly, that is to say, a common-law one. Again, Meredith shows his own approval of the arrangement, this time through Matthew's insistence that their relationship does not offend 'Divine law' (*LO* 28; 332). When a strange twist of events brings Ormont himself in contact with them abroad, even he accepts their union. He and Lady Charlotte have come to see a progressive, international Swiss boarding-school that they have learnt of, that might suit Lady Charlotte's grandson. Meredith is perfectly Victorian in his recourse to coincidence, and this turns out to be the very school that Matthew and Aminta are running. However, the visitors like the place, and see that the boys there are being brought on nicely: there has been no such 'tatterdemalion of shipwreck', no such 'rueful exhibition of ideas put to the business of life', as Ormont had anticipated for Matthew when he left his employ (*LO* 26; 310). So the visitors choose not to reveal the irregularity of the young couple's relationship; instead of starting a scandal that might have closed the school, they enrol the boy there. In a further stroke of luck, Ormont dies six months later, giving Matthew and Aminta the opportunity denied to Victor Radnor and Nataly – to tie the knot according to society's laws.

No doubt this serves as a reward for Matthew's vision as an educator, which shares centre stage in the novel with the couple's love for each other. The only problem is that Aminta's development suffers from the shift of emphasis. Once the school was expected to be mixed, and she had imagined teaching alongside Matthew: 'She had lessons to give to girls, she had sympathy, pity, anticipation' (*LO* 16; 201). But in the event, only boys are mentioned, and when the pair are worrying about how Ormont will react to finding them, Aminta tells Matthew, 'I am fit to be the school-housekeeper; for nothing else' (*LO* 30; 352). By 'nothing else' she means 'no other way of life'; but she still refers to herself in a domestic rather than a teaching capacity. For the heroine as an independent entity, this seems a rather disappointing conclusion to her story.

*

Still, Meredith's heroines go out on a high note with the stalwart Carinthia in the novel actually entitled *The Amazing Marriage*. Nursing is one of the very few ways, like singing (Emilia), writing (Diana) and teaching (Aminta – had she really done it), for a woman to act in the larger world. From early on, we learn, Carinthia has it in mind to become a nurse. Representing 'a new idea of women' (*AM* 8; 80), she first appears as a big-hearted, still tomboyish young woman, her affinity with nature never clearer than when she climbs a forest tree while her future husband Lord Fleetwood trembles for her safety. When Fleetwood mistreats her as a newly-wed, she finds her way to the East End, and later stays with Owain Wytham and his invalid wife Rebecca in Wales – where Fleetwood owns mines, and is Owain's employer. More mature now, and the mother of Fleetwood's child, she feels for the miners and their families during a strike; in one harrowing episode she confronts a mad dog and deals unflinchingly with the little boy it has bitten (though, typically, the cauterizing of the bite takes place off-stage). We see that she is beginning to realize her ambition to nurse, and indeed she later accompanies her brother to Spain, where she tends the wounded on both sides in the Carlist civil war. But perhaps the most impressive thing she does is simply to resist the eventually remorseful Fleetwood's overtures to her. Thus, another egoist is taught the error of his ways. It is a hard lesson. Fleetwood is not such a bad man: rather like Victor Radnor, he is more thoughtless than wicked and he takes up the monastic life in the end, punishing himself to death with austerities. But his repentance comes too late for Carinthia; she will not allow herself to be possessed again. In keeping with Meredith's idea of the shapely life, she does remarry after

'Brother Russet's' death. However, her new husband is Owain, more or less bequeathed to her when Rebecca died, and, with his dog-like devotion, he promises to be more her follower than her leader. Not only has the old kind of hero been squashed, but the new kind has dwindled, and the heroine reigns supreme.

Even by Meredith's standards, this last complete novel is a challenging read. He employs all his customary techniques here to probe his main characters' psychology and present his own ideas, in a narrative using the chatty 'Dame Gossip' as a chorus (as he puts it himself, in the title of Chapter 1); a wandering Welshman called Gower Woodseer, full of gnomic utterances about nature and women; interpolated letters; and such long internal debates as Lord Fleetwood's, when he puzzles over his feelings for his wife in Chapter 37. The plot is also much more complicated than appears here, and takes, perhaps even more so than usual,[15] the postmodernist form of a loose chain of events. 'Character must ever be a mystery', declares the narrator in the very last paragraph, proving Meredith's awareness of what he has been doing, 'only to be explained in some degree by conduct; and that is very dependent upon accident'. Just as unpredictable is his style, which veers alarmingly between the turgidly mannerist and the impressionistically staccatto.[16] Yet Carinthia towers above it all, drawn on the same kind of epic scale as Vittoria, but with more grip of her own destiny. Few will forget her confrontation with Fleetwood, when he tries to stop her helping the bitten child: 'It is life and death, and I must not be commanded', she cries (*AM* 33; 342). The rewards of reading this highly experimental novel are at least commensurate with the effort required from the reader.

*

'It's a woman, old girl, that makes me / Think more kindly of the race', says Juggling Jerry to his wife in Meredith's poem of that title. She could have ruled palaces, Jerry feels, but she chose a hard life with him. Right to the end, Meredith was fascinated by strong women, and keeps us fascinated by them too. Indeed, the signs are that the heroine of his incomplete *Celt and Saxon* would have been one of his most charismatic heroines yet – a girl of 'glorious beauty and great-heartedness' (*CS* 6; 47) who illumines 'an expanded world... miraculous, yet the real one, only wanting such light to show its riches' (CS 7; 51). So far, Adiante has appeared only by report and in her miniature likeness, but that simply raises expectation. It is obvious that her creator has maintained an unflagging belief in women's capacity for strength and nobility – and in the special part they can play both in social evolution, and the operations of 'our mild prevailing ancient mother nature' (CS 6; 43). Meredith's good friend, the radical liberal John Morley, claimed at the time that 'the stir of all the table-talk about his gallery of fair ladies' contributed to 'far-reaching social discussion'.[17] Without doubt, in his own way and for his own reasons, Meredith was one of the staunchest, most influential 'male feminists' of the age.

6

The Later Poetry

Even at his busiest, Meredith had continued to publish poems in periodicals, including substantial ones like 'France, December 1870', his stern exhortation to the beleaguered French ('Now is humanity on trial in thee') at the time of the Franco-Prussian War.[1] Since his mid-50s he had been devoting more time to poetry, revising and extending 'Love in the Valley', adding the prefatory sonnet to 'Modern Love', and publishing five new volumes of verse. Here as in the novels he aims to illuminate 'an expanded world' for others, as Adiante is said to do in *Celt and Saxon*. Drawn as ever to epic subjects, he sometimes attempts this through character and action, notably in *Ballads and Poems of Tragic Life* (1887). Indeed, the poet George MacBeth thought that 'his best work is in his dramatic pieces',[2] such as the long 'Nuptials of Attila' and the shorter 'King Harald's Trance' – both from this volume, both ending in tragedy and confusion, and both with a woman as one of the victims. Even if Attila's reluctant new slave-bride was responsible for his death, and even if King Harald's treacherous and unfaithful wife deserved her fate, their ends seem pitiable. The scene in which King Harald suddenly sits bolt upright in his bed, kisses his sword, rises to his feet and slays his pregnant queen is particularly horrific, especially since he then doubles up and dies at his war-chiefs' feet before he can slay her lover. Predictably, such poems were too much for Sassoon, who says of the former, 'My soul craves for something gentler than "arrow, javelin, spear and sword"',[3] and despite MacBeth's praise they are not much read today.

In the more meditative poems, as in the novels as a whole, the aim is to encourage the reader to transcend the self, to reach out towards fellow human beings and upwards towards nature. The struggle here is still dramatic, but the drama is expressed in terms of life/death, light/dark imagery, and with reference to an even vaster time-scale – for this is the struggle not of an individual, a couple, or even a country at some point in history, but of the human race itself. Some of these poems have lasted better. This being the case, Meredith's verse has generally been perceived as philosophical, didactic, or at best 'descriptive-doctrinal'.[4] Wendell Harris suggests severe 'winnowings' to preserve the most appealing and accessible of the poems, recommending the exclusion of all the poetry of the last seventeen years, and much else besides.[5] Graham Hough and Keith Hanley, who respectively edited two twentieth-century selections, focus on 'Modern Love' and just a handful of others, such as 'Love in the Valley' and a few from *Poems and Lyrics of the Joy of Earth* (1883). Hanley also includes several from *A Reading of Earth* (1888). But both omit the important four-part 'Woods of Westermain' from the former volume, suggesting that they have missed the point about the later poetry. Like all Meredith's work, including 'Modern Love', this part of his *oeuvre* is not heavily moralistic. On the contrary, it is best seen as exploratory and participatory – that is, as personal experience recreated for the reader to share.[6]

'The Druid's Grove, Norbury Park: Ancient Yew Trees' by Thomas Allom, in E. W. Brayley's *A Topographical History of Surrey*, Vol. IV (Willis, 1851), facing p.453

Inspired by Meredith's beloved Druid's Grove,[7] 'The Woods of Westermain' exemplifies the kind of poetry Meredith was most engaged with in these last years, and, challenging as it is, comes closest to making his mature vision explicit. As in Milton's paired 'L'Allegro' and 'Il Penseroso', hypnotically rhythmic seven-syllable lines beckon us into a world with the potential to be seen from two entirely different points of view. The mysterious depths of nature, seething with life and movement, are delightful to those who are open to experience: 'Toss your heart up with the lark, / Foot at peace with mouse and worm' (WW I). But to the apprehensive, the distrustful, they are threatening: 'All the eyeballs under hoods / Shroud you in their glare' (WW II). This duality is then explored in two much longer parts. As for the receptive,

> Farther, deeper, may you read,
> Have you sight for things afield,
> Where peeps she, the Nurse of seed,
> Cloaked, but in the peep revealed;
> Showing a kind face and sweet:
> Look you with the soul you see't,
> Glory narrowing to grace,
> Grace to glory magnified,
> Following that will you embrace
> Close in arms or aëry wide.

(WW III)

Here, the 'Nurse of seed' is of course evolving nature, a power to be welcomed, a power to enrich the spirit. But again, for those who bring in 'a note / Wrangling', everything is different. They will not hear the pipings of Pan, or see the 'lustreful' foliage or 'the huntress moon / radiantly facing dawn'; nor will they achieve a 'larger self' through such experiences, or enter into fellowship with the like-minded, or find love. Instead, they will be mired in a world of bestiality, cruelty and oppression, a world of which Meredith has always been only too aware.[8] For these sojourners, 'Nightmare upon horror broods' (WW III); owls screech and spectres haunt them. Of the many darker images and symbols woven through the poem, such as the 'moth-winged jar' (WW II), snakes, owls, the serpent and the tiger, the most important is that of the dragon, which suggests not so much self as the pride in self that is the root of all ills, and must be jettisoned. As explained in the last and longest part, the trick is to 'love the light so well / That no darkness will seem fell'. Then, no such phantoms or monsters will appear. What is seen instead is only the play of light, which symbolizes life itself in continual healthful movement:

> Then you touch the nerve of Change
> Then of Earth you have the clue;
> Then her two-sexed meanings melt
> Through you, wed the thought and felt.
>
> (WW IV)

Meredith's ideas blend seamlessly here as he both experiences and suggests the reward of accepting change, of absorbing it into the mind and the sensations. Curiously, this reward is spiritual calm, a kind of permanence that is quite different from static sameness or fixity:

> Lo, you look at Flow and Drought
> Interflashed and interwrought:
> Ended is begun, begun
> Ended, quick as torrents run.
>
> . . . .
>
> Look with spirit past the sense,
> Spirit shines in permanence.
>
> (WW IV)

Harmony with others and with the world at large has been seen as a major goal throughout Meredith's work. In order to be fully alive, in order to achieve 'true felicity', integration needs to occur within the self as well. 'Blood and brain and spirit' have to come together:

> Earth that Triad is: she hides
> Joy from him who that divides;
> Showers it when the three are one
> Glassing her in union.
>
> (WW IV)

'Glassing', with its suggestion of light passing through and being contained, is the perfect word here. Meredith fully acknowledges the stern realities of life in this poem, but chooses to see and work for the brighter possibilities, recommending the same process to his readers. Entering the 'enchanted woods' is still a challenge, even at the end, where the refrain ('Enter these enchanted woods / You who dare') is repeated for the last time. But it is one for which he has tried to prepare us.

In contrast to the owl, night-jar, vulture and horrible 'scaly Dragon-fowl' (WW IV) that swoop through the shadows of 'The Woods of Westermain', the songbird rises, chirps and flutters through the daylight, and also expresses the joyous soul within. Meredith takes up this idea again in 'The Lark Ascending', with its memorably accurate mimetic opening:

> He rises and begins to round,
> He drops the silver chain of sound,
> Of many links without a break,
> In chirrup, whistle, slur and shake,
> All intervolved and spreading wide,
> Like water-dimples down a tide
> Where ripple ripple overcurls
> And eddy into eddy whirls;

This first sentence is a *tour de force* that lasts the whole verse paragraph of 64 lines. But the simple point is that the bird, as he says in 'The Woods of Westermain' (WW III) is 'bird and more', calling forth the best in us 'to him akin', that is to say, the human spirit freed from 'taint of personality' and hence egoism, spiralling widely upwards to enrich the world – extending it 'at wings and dome' for others.[9]

The best poems of these years carry us naturally from images to philosophical ideas in a similar way,[10] striking a balance between concrete and abstract. This is movingly achieved through the light conditions and personifications of what G. M. Trevelyan considered to be 'one of his greatest poems',[11] 'Hymn to Colour'. The scene here is set at the break of day, when 'night puts away / Her darker veil for grey', progressing to when 'Colour, the soul's bridegroom, makes / The house of heaven splendid for the bride'. During this time, the speaker, who has been walking between Life and Death, and who has been guided by Love, conceives a state in which body and soul are in harmony – where men, '[n]ot forfeiting the beast with which they are crossed' attain to the 'stature of the Gods'. Uplifted by this intimation, the speaker finally sees the dawn 'glow through' even Death itself. A similar balance and epiphany is achieved in 'In the Woods'. Derived like 'Dirge in

Woods' from an earlier, longer poem of about 1870 ('In the Woods: Foresight and Patience'), this is a sequence of six short lyrics in which Meredith again adopts the time-honoured allegory of life as journey. Trampling weeds and touching the furrowed bark of the trees, the speaker here makes the same choice that Robert Frost's speaker does later, in one of the best-known poems of the next century, 'Stopping By Woods on a Snowy Evening'. That is, he decides to continue his journey rather than sink into the darkness.[12] But Meredith's speaker makes his choice in a very different spirit. His decision 'to proceed / By the light I have within' comes from the sheer love of life rather than from any sense of duty. Not that he clings frantically to life, or even to the hope of an after-life. 'Like a ring for the bride', he simply holds life in his hand, and is ready to be generous with it. Nothing could be more essentially Meredithian.

Some of the longer poems of these years are less coherent, even though they started out as independent pieces. Even the expanded 'Love in the Valley', which has many fine new lines, suffers from a disconnection between its piled-up images and the yearning for 'heaven' in the last stanza. This produces a far weaker ending than the earlier version's ringing cry: 'Lo! The nest is ready, let me not languish longer! / Bring her to my arms on the first May night'. More damagingly, despite being inspired by the very bird that sings outside his study window and recalls his own youth to him, 'The Thrush in February' soon vanishes into a thicket of evolutionary ideas. No longer thrilling to a simple union with nature, Meredith maintains here that the 'beast' must indeed be forfeited, if 'the tidal multitude and blind' are to be led by the heroes amongst us 'from bestial to the higher breed'.[13] The abstractions Love, Pleasures, Pains, Life and Death all vie for our consideration in a single quatrain (stanza 38), long after the 'twilight bird' is last mentioned. Again, the impact of the original experience is lost.

'The rapture of the forward view', as Meredith puts it in 'The Thrush in February', is easier for him to sustain in shorter lyrics like 'The Orchard and the Heath'. Here as elsewhere, he had been doing his own 'winnowing': when printed in *Macmillan's Magazine* in early 1868, this was followed by another hundred lines of reflection. But the stanzas as they appear in *Poems and*

Lyrics of the Joy of Earth are complete enough, and wonderfully evocative. On a long walk, the speaker sees children playing in an orchard. Their world is a carefree world of plenty: 'They had but to lift hands or wait / For fruits to fill them; fruits were all their sky'. Later in the day though, past the 'pleasant farms and lanes' and across the heath, the speaker comes upon a gypsy encampment under a 'patched channel-bank' overrun with late foxgloves. Here he sees some more children, including three girls poised to race each other, 'with shoulders like a boat at sea / Tipped sideways by the wave'. As the girls bend forward, their ragged clothes slide sideways off their shoulders 'from either ridge unequally' – a slightly provocative detail that reminds us of Harry Richmond and his unfettered Kiomi. The girls' brothers egg them on, but suddenly smell wood-smoke and lose interest in their sport. They stretch out by the camp-fire instead, where a dog waits eagerly too, 'upright in circle', as supper comes to the boil. Both these scenes, in the orchard and the gipsy camp, evoke youth, energy and natural appetite under the changing heavens. But, having made clear the contrasts in the children's lots, the observer seems wistful at the end, his appreciation of earth's riches tinged with the glow of sunset. In Part 2 of the poem, as originally printed, he had gone on to wish for 'equal destinies' for the children, a goal to be achieved through the 'service' of the better-placed.[14]

There is never anything facile about Meredith's glad receptiveness to natural energies. As for his own lot, by now he has had more than his share of 'thwackings' from life, and *A Reading of Earth*, published not long after his wife's painful illness and death, shows just how much he struggled to come to terms with this latest blow. 'Change in Recurrence' gives a particularly moving picture of his lonely life at this time:

> I stood at the gate of the cot
> Where my darling, with side-glance demure,
> Would spy, on her trim garden-plot,
> The busy wild things chase and lure.
> . . . . . .
> I gazed: 'twas the scene of the frame,
> With the face, the dear life for me, fled.
>
> (I; III)

He had never shirked the fact and prospect of mortality, and he is not, in the end, overwhelmed either by his bereavement or by his own approaching death. Back in 1862, in 'Ode to the Spirit of Earth in Autumn', he had asked nature: 'Teach me to feel myself the tree, / And not the withered leaf', and this request seems to have been granted. As late as 1892, in *Poems: The Empty Purse, with Odes to the Comic Spirit, to Youth in Memory, and Verses*, the 'lyre of earth' still plays for him in 'Night of Frost in May'. And in his very last collection of 1901, *A Reading of Life with Other Poems*, even as he endures his solitariness, grows deafer still and loses his mobility, he poignantly expresses and communicates to us in 'Song in the Songless' his unwearied response to life:

> They have no song, the sedges dry,
>   And still they sing.
> It is within my breast they sing,
>   As I pass by.

'George Meredith aet 72', from a dry-point etching by Mortimer Menpes (frontispiece to the Memorial Edition of *Diana of the Crossways*, Vol. 16)

CONCLUSION

Like Laetitia Dale in *The Egoist*, Meredith had once dreamt of 'conquering the world with a pen' (*E* 16; 130), but for many years had been disappointed. He blamed this on having been ahead of his times: 'it is the way with the English to drub a purveyor of new wares for thirty years', he complained in old age, specifying the very time-gap between *Shagpat* and *Diana of the Crossways*, 'after which they worship him' (*SL*, 155). But his early struggles were indeed rewarded now, if not by hordes of readers, at least by notable ones. Arthur Conan Doyle was proved right when he said in the *National Review* that 'Meredith was made to be imitated' (*CH*, 330). Apprentice writers began striking out right and left from the new paths he had trodden for them. The young Lawrence revered him, responding to the 'beautiful pristine fervour' of Richard Feverel, and feeling it 'presumptuous' to mention himself in the same breath as his creator.[15] Meredith's ideas about the integration of blood, brain and spirit, and the dynamic onward processes of life, of which both sex and death were an inevitable part, found their natural heir in the young northerner. James Joyce took something from individual episodes in Meredith's novels,[16] but also, more importantly, from his strenuous efforts to probe his characters' mental processes and emotions, and to represent them, often brokenly, on the page. Not the only source of inspiration for the stream-of-consciousness technique developed by Joyce and Woolf, Meredith was nevertheless one of those sources. As for the poetry, there are echoes of his imagery in the works of Hardy himself – in the 'tangled bine-stems' and 'broken lyres' of Hardy's 'The Darkling Thrush' of 1900, as well as of his intimation of hope in a difficult world, though it is that poignant note of 'Dirge in Woods', 'Change in Recurrence' and 'Song in the Songless' that comes through in Hardy's *Poems of 1912–13* after his first wife Emma's death. W. B. Yeats's idea of 'delight in the whole man – blood, imagination, intellect, running together'[17] also, surely, owes much to Meredith. Even T. S. Eliot famously lifted the climactic line of his early poem 'Cousin Nancy' ('The army of unalterable law'), from 'Lucifer in Starlight', Meredith's powerful sonnet of 1883, in which he gives a cosmic view of Lucifer's inevitable fall.[18]

What might have pleased Meredith most, with his growing sense of the limited power of words, is that many passages of his poems were set to music, or inspired instrumental pieces, notably Ralph Vaughan Williams's much-loved 'The Lark Ascending'. It is sometimes seen as ironic that Hardy's sonnet 'George Meredith, 1828–1909' should have prophesied his future influence, but it is not: Meredith's words do live on 'further and further still, / Through the world's vaporous vitiate air', without our always realizing it. This seems a fitting legacy for a man who tried so valiantly to combat self-pride and who reached out to life with such unfailing generosity of spirit.

Notes

INTRODUCTION

1. See John Lucas on the 'catastrophic collapse' of his reputation in 'Meredith's Reputation' (Norton, 549), and John Sutherland on him as a 'Revered Corpse', *Times Literary Supplement* (5 September 1997): 5.
2. Quoted from Lady Milner's radio talk on him in 'George Meredith: Lover of Life and Laughter', *The Times*, 7 June 1937, 21 (Lady Milner was his friend Frederick Maxse's daughter).
3. See Sally Ledger, *The New Woman: Fiction and Feminism at the Fin de Siècle* (Manchester: Manchester University Press, 1997), 134.
4. Lafcadio Hearn, *Pre-Raphaelites and Other Poets: Lectures*, ed. John Erskine (New York: Dodd, Mead, 1922), 312–13. See also Bonamy Dobrée, *The Broken Cistern: The Clark Lectures, 1952–53* (Cohen & West, 1954), 94.
5. Meredith's own instincts differed from, and could even be opposed to, those of 'the French philosopher' (*The Egoist* 10; 80): in the 1840s, for example, Comte reacted to a radical workers' movement by turning towards the right – not something the unrepentant 'Old Chartist' in Meredith's *'Modern Love' and Poems of the English Roadside*, or Dr Shrapnel in *Beauchamp's Career*, would have countenanced.

CHAPTER 1. A LIFE IN STAGES

1. He rode to hounds, became a Freemason, joined the Portsmouth Yeomanry Cavalry, etc., not always bothering to bill illustrious clients; Rear Admiral Sir Thomas Hardy stayed at his house. See S. M. Ellis's *George Meredith: His Life and Friends in Relation to His Work* (Grant Richards, 1920, 2nd ed.), 24, 33, and Lionel Stevenson's *The Ordeal of George Meredith* (Peter Owen, 1954), 5.

2. See Mervyn Jones, *The Amazing Victorian: A Life of George Meredith* (Constable, 1999), 24.
3. See Stevenson, *The Ordeal of George Meredith*, 11.
4. See J. S. L. Pulford's *George & Mary Meredith in Weybridge, Shepperton & Esher, 1849–61*. Walton & Weybridge Local History Society: Paper No. 27, 1989, 1–2.
5. For reasons for his apparently leaving Neuwied early, see Ellis, *George Meredith*, 54 (his inheritance may have been reduced by bad investments); on confusion about his date of return, see *SL*, 17–18n.
6. Georg Roppen, correctly I think, finds Meredith's 'God' to be a 'synthesis of various ideologies...Idealism, pantheism, evolution, positivism and the religion of humanity', in *Evolution and Poetic Belief: A Study in Some Victorian and Modern Writers* (Oslo: Oslo University Press, 1956), 277.
7. Siegfried Sassoon, *Meredith* (Grey Arrow, 1959), 15.
8. See Nicholas Joukovsky, 'According to Mrs Bennet', *Times Literary Supplement* (8 October 2004): 15.
9. Both are mentioned in David Williams's *George Meredith: His Life and Lost Love* (Hamish Hamilton, 1977), 29.
10. William Sharp, 'The Country of George Meredith', *Selected Writings, Vol. IV, Literary Geography and Travel-Sketches* (Heinemann, 1912), 57–8.
11. Joukovsky believes this is what 'cost Meredith the love and respect of his wife' ('According to Mrs Bennet', 15).
12. See another article by Joukovsky, 'Mary Ellen's First Affair: New Light on the Biographical Background to *Modern Love*' in *Times Literary Supplement* (15 June 2007), 13–15.
13. See particularly Pulford, *George & Mary Meredith*, 27, and Williams, *George Meredith*, 41, for her complex state of mind around this time.
14. Sassoon, *Meredith*, 64.
15. Quoted in Stevenson, *The Ordeal of George Meredith*, 81–2.
16. A difficult process. See Cline's 'The Betrothal of George Meredith to Marie Vulliamy' in *Nineteenth-Century Fiction* 16/3 (December 1961): 231–43.
17. Quoted in 'The Love Letters of a Novelist', *Penny Illustrated Paper*, 3 August 1912, 159.
18. Edward Mendelson, introduction to *The Ordeal of Richard Feverel* (Penguin, 1998), xi.
19. See Flora Thompson's *Heatherley* (Headley Down: John Owen Smith, 2005), 34.
20. In this (file 2424 in the Surrey History Centre, Woking), Meredith expresses gratitude on hearing of an effort to publicize his work (i.e. a lecture on it) in Plymouth.
21. 'The King's Sympathy', *The Times*, 21 May 1909, 8.

22. Barrie's tribute in the *Westminster Gazette* later appeared as *Neither Dorking Nor the Abbey: George Meredith (1828–1909)* (Chicago: Browne's Bookstore, 1910). The funeral was movingly reported in *The Times* of 24 May 1902, 12.

CHAPTER 2. *POEMS* (1851) AND 'MODERN LOVE'

1. Quoted in S. M. Ellis, *George Meredith: His Life and Friends in Relation to His Work* (Grant Richards, 1920, 2nd ed.), 281.
2. William Hardman, *A Mid-Victorian Pepys: The Letters and Memoirs of Sir William Hardman, MA FRGS*, ed. S. M. Ellis (Cecil Palmer, 1923), 50.
3. Quoted in *The Poems of George Meredith*, ed. Phyllis Bartlett, 2 vols (New York: Yale University Press, 1978), I: 25.
4. See Lionel Stevenson, *The Ordeal of George Meredith* (Peter Owen, 1954), 39.
5. N.B. Classical influence pervades these early poems, including 'Love in the Valley'. See John von B. Rodenbeck's 'The Classicism of Meredith's "Love in the Valley"' in *Victorian Poetry* 11/1 (Spring 1973): 27–37.
6. e.g., when Clara is about to flee Willoughby in *The Egoist*, the narrator comments: 'Our design shapes us for the work in hand, the passions man the ship, the position is their apology: and now should conscience be a passenger on board, a merely seeming swiftness of our vessel will keep him dumb as the unwilling guest of a pirate captain scudding from the cruiser half in cloven brine through rocks and shoals to save his black flag.' (25; 204). Meredith often gets carried away by the sea.
7. Bartlett points out Tennyson's influence here in *Poems* II: 1136, but this was already very much part of his own optimistic world view.
8. Isobel Armstrong, *Victorian Poetry, Poetics and Politics* (Routledge, 1993), 459.
9. Quoted in Ellis, *George Meredith*, 281.
10. Wendell Harris, for example, puts it in a class of its own, claiming that its exploration of the inner life 'challenges Meredith's explicit philosophy as found in the poems of earth'. See 'Sorting and Sifting Meredith's Poetry' in Richard A. Levine, ed., *The Victorian Experience: Poets* (Athens, Oh.: Ohio University Press, 1982), 135.
11. Section V, 'Frederick to his Mother'. As Armstrong says, the wife in 'Modern Love' is more 'the witch or the Medusa in the house' than the Angel (p. 437).
12. 'Not dead? Not yet quite dead?', *Othello*, 5.ii.85. Cf. references to *Othello* in *The Egoist*, where Mrs Mountstuart Jenkinson warns

Clara that Willoughby's 'vengeance in anticipation of an imagined offence' might take the form of reciprocal unfaithfulness (35; 291) – another clue to the situation here.
13. Lucas finds 'intended badnesses' in the narrator, mainly in the opening sonnets. See 'Meredith as Poet' in Ian Fletcher, ed., *Meredith Now: Some Critical Essays* (Routledge & Kegan Paul, 1971), 23.
14. *Astrophil and Stella* XLV. Reader analyses Meredith's own author/narrator/husband nexus in 'The Autobiographical Author as Fictional Character: Point of View in Meredith's "Modern Love"', *Victorian Poetry* 10/2 (1972): 131–43.
15. Preface, *Modern Love: George Meredith*, ed. Gillian Beer (Syrens [Penguin], 1998), viii. But Beer suggests this is because of the 'game' element here.
16. Norman Friedman includes this in the 'midnight-tomb-ghost-skeleton-grave-shadow' image-cluster in the sequence, though it also links with the 'murder-knife-wound-blood' one. Many of these dark, painful images overlap like this; categorizing them is not very helpful. See 'The Jangled Harp: Symbolic Structure in *Modern Love*', *Modern Language Quarterly* 18 (1957): 13.
17. See Michael Lund's 'Space and Spiritual Crisis in Meredith's *Modern Love*' in *Victorian Poetry* 16/4 (Winter 1978): 376–82, though Lund's highly negative reading rests on an acknowledged inability to interpret the symbolism at the end ('Whatever those "ramping hosts" suggest as symbols', 382). N.B. Meredith often expressed his distaste for cynicism, e.g. in *The Egoist* (7; 54).
18. See *Poems*, ed. Bartlett II: 1138n.
19. A strange reading in Lucas's 'Meredith as Poet', 32.
20. The 'golden harp' in this poem links it to 'Ode to the Spirit of Earth in Autumn', where such a harp 'is struck once more / And all its music is for me!'

CHAPTER 3. THE FIRST 'THWACKINGS': FROM *THE SHAVING OF SHAGPAT* TO *THE ADVENTURES OF HARRY RICHMOND*

1. In *Shagpat*, too, Shibli has a phial and a magic lily. Perhaps Meredith was inspired here by Charles Mansfield's real-life researches, one of which concerned perfuming soap, as well as by the real Giovanni Maria Farina's invention of *eau de Cologne* in the early eighteenth century.
2. Susan Payne argues convincingly for his 'iconoclastic treatment of the Bildungsroman mode' in *Difficult Discourse: George Meredith's Experimental Fiction* (Pisa: ETS, 1995), 28.

3. See Mervyn Jones, *The Amazing Victorian: A Life of George Meredith* (Constable, 1999), 74.
4. Milan Kundera, *The Art of the Novel* (Faber, 1986), 144–5.
5. Sandoe, so witheringly dismissed in the novel, is of course the Henry Wallis figure here.
6. Such as Helen Huntingdon in Anne Brontë's *The Tenant of Wildfell Hall*, who also wants to protect her son Arthur from temptation: 'I will lead him by the hand...till he has strength to go alone' (Oxford: Oxford University Press, World's Classics, 1906), 22.
7. e.g., in Herbert Spencer's essay, 'Moral Development', the child is seen as developing his higher moral faculties only when the time is ripe. Cf. the narrator's comment here, 'Conscience was beginning to inhabit him' (12; 93).
8. Sir Austin himself acknowledges that a 'maker of proverbs' is 'a narrow mind the mouthpiece of a narrower', though Lady Blandish suspects this is a case of false humility (44; 521).
9. Even the aptly named Mountfalcon and Bella Mount escape being stage villains – both come to respect the goodness in their respective 'prey'.
10. Ironically, as a character in her own right, Clare has been much neglected. But see Sally Shuttleworth's *The Mind of the Child: Child Development in Literature, Science, and Medicine, 1830-1900* (Oxford: Oxford University Press, 2010) for Meredith's unusual understanding of her needs, and the damage done by her 'self-suppression' (p. 174).
11. Taken together, Austin Wentworth, Lady Blandish and Mrs Berry counterbalance the human failings exposed in the novel, as Lucy does the misogyny. Mrs Berry's overdone soft-heartedness shows Meredith falling into the sentimentalism he himself deplored – but Lady Blandish finds in her *'twice* the sense of anyone' (44; 555).
12. Edward Mendelson, Introduction to *The Ordeal of Richard Feverel* (Penguin, 1998), xxiv.
13. Sassoon, as a writer himself, thinks too much is made of this, and that Meredith simply transformed 'the personal dilemma of his origin...into a grand opportunity for a serio-comic extravaganza'. He concedes though that Meredith may have been working off a 'lurking resentment' about his origins (*Meredith* (Grey Arrow, 1959), 53).
14. For a fuller discussion, see Marie Banfield's *'Evan Harrington, The Adventures of Harry Richmond,* and the Evolutionary Debate of the 1860s' in the Victorian Web, at <http://www.victorianweb.org/authors/meredith/banfield1.html>.
15. On 'peripheralism' here in general, see David Howard's 'Meredith in the Margin' in Ian Fletcher's collection, *Meredith Now: Some*

Critical Essays (Routledge & Kegan Paul, 1971), 131 ff. Renate Muendel in *George Meredith* (Boston: Twayne, 1986), 74, finds Rhoda herself 'unusually static' and 'peripheral' for a heroine.
16. An anonymous reviewer in 'The New Meredith', *The Daily News*, 15 April 1897. N.B. Meredith himself said later that *'Rhoda Fleming* is liked by some, not much by me' (*SL*, 197).
17. Howard, 'Meredith in the Margin', 130.
18. e.g. see the opening of Chapter 88 in Trollope's contemporaneous *He Knew He Was Right* (1868–9).
19. See Gillian Beer, in *Meredith: A Change of Masks: A Study of the Novels* (Athlone Press, 1970), 172–3; also Allon White, *The Uses of Obscurity: The Fiction of Early Modernism* (Routledge & Kegan Paul, 1981), 27, on the 'dialogic' tension thus produced.
20. On Mazzini's ideas, see Marie Banfield's 'Meredith, Mazzini and the *Risorgimento*: The Italian Novels' in *RSV* (*Revista di Studi Vittoriani*) 11/21 (January 2006): 58.
21. For Roy Richmond's association with fire and its general role in the novel, whether destructive, purgatorial or simply exciting, see Barbara Hardy's *The Appropriate Form* (Athlone Press, 1964), 92–6.

CHAPTER 4. A NEW KIND OF HERO: FROM *BEAUCHAMP'S CAREER* TO *THE EGOIST*

1. Siegfried Sassoon, *Meredith* (Grey Arrow, 1959), 151.
2. 'Sometimes *Harry Richmond* is my favourite, but I am inclined to give the palm to *Beauchamp's Career*. There is a breezy, human interest about it, and the plot here has a consistency and logical development which *Feverel* lacks...' (quoted in S. M. Ellis, *George Meredith: His Life and Friends in Relation to His Work* (Grant Richards, 1920, 2nd ed.), 241). He was also flattered that French critics admired his portrait of Renée. David Williams too considers *Beauchamp's Career* 'the first, and greatest, of his more deeply personal books' (*George Meredith: His Life and Lost Love* (Hamish Hamilton, 1977), 128).
3. Richard C. Stevenson, *The Experimental Impulse in George Meredith's Fiction* (Lewisburg, Penn.: Bucknell University Press, 2004), 53. On the mix of ideals currently in vogue, see my own 'The Impossible Goal: The Struggle for Manhood in Victorian Fiction' in *The Victorian Newsletter* 89 (Spring 1996): 1–10. The Carlylean idea of the gamely, indomitably struggling hero seems uppermost here, e.g. see *Carlyle's Lectures on Heroes Hero-Worship and the Heroic in History*, ed. P. C. Parr (Oxford: Clarendon, 1910), 42. Meredith, who

had met Carlyle, was as great a fan of his as Maxse (see Sassoon, *Meredith*, 36–7, 39).
4. Much as he had caught a fever after distributing food in the French camp in Chapter 4. See Barbara Hardy on Meredith's 'habit of repetition' as shown in *Harry Richmond* (*The Appropriate Form* (Athlone Press, 1964), 96). This applies to whole patterns of behaviour across the *oeuvre*, from duelling to 'thwackings' to hero-worship – as for the latter, here for instance, unlike others, Nevil sees nothing ridiculous about Dr Shrapnel.
5. Nevil's raving, and Shrapnel's hysterical chuckles when Romfrey comes to visit him, are disconcerting. Like the nonsense syllables interpolated into Mrs Berry's last speech in *Richard Feverel* when she comforts Lucy's baby, they may show Meredith struggling against sentimentalism. They may also reflect his awareness of how readers might react to such characters. Here, for instance, he well knew that 'Liberal and Radical sentiment is shared by a very minor portion' (*Letters* 2: 588). For the presence of the reader 'at the heart of his creative act', see Judith Wilt's *The Readable People of George Meredith* (Princeton: Princeton University Press, 1975), 5.
6. Thus he dies in a similar manner to Mary Ellen's first husband, an event so significant for Meredith's first marriage that it must always have stayed in his mind. Elements of Nicolls, a 'dashing tearaway' (Williams, *George Meredith*, 21), as well as of Maxse, can be found in Nevil.
7. Although Darwin preferred words like self-sacrifice, benevolence etc. to the Comtean term. See Banfield, 'Meredith's Altruist: Evolution and Politics' in *Beauchamp's Career: George Meredith: Testo e Contesto*, ed. Anna Enrichetta Soccio (Rome: Aracne, 2008), 83, n.18.
8. In *George Meredith: His Life and Work* (Bodley Head, 1956), 220, the influential Marxist critic Jack Lindsay claims it shows an 'anguished desire for union with the Common man'; but it can also be seen as 'a dramatic illustration of the Young England doctrine that the generous idealism of the aristocracy can come to the rescue of the common people' (Mervyn Jones, *The Amazing Victorian: A Life of George Meredith* (Constable, 1999), 190). Meredith had certainly been interested in the New England Movement in the 1850s and 1860s – Norman Kelvin discusses his Tory leanings in *A Troubled Eden: Nature and Society in the Works of George Meredith* (Stanford: Stanford University Press, 1968), 11–14. Either of these views seems preferable to Frederick Karl's totally negative reading, that Nevil 'dies immolated in a swirl of exhausted ideals', in '*Beauchamp's Career*: An English Ordeal', *Nineteenth-Century Fiction* 16/2 (September 1961): 131.

NOTES

9. James S. Stone, *George Meredith's Politics: As Seen in his Life, Friendships and Works* (Oakville, Ont.: P. D. Meany, 1986), 4. Note however that Meredith did not consider the 'satiric rod' to be a pure form of the Comic Spirit ('Essay on Comedy', 444).
10. See Charles J. Hill's 'The Portrait of the Author in *Beauchamp's Career*' in *Journal of English and Germanic Philology* 52/3 (July 1953): 332–9. Margaret Harris in her introduction to the World's Classics edition (1988), xiii, has another candidate for the model: Edward Hearne, a very radical Southampton doctor.
11. David Howard, 'George Meredith: "Delicate" and "Epical" Fiction' in John Lucas, ed., *Literature and Politics in the Nineteenth Century* (Methuen, 1971), 168.
12. It has long been felt that 'he placed too much faith in the status quo' (Gillian Beer, *Meredith: A Change of Masks: A Study of the Novels* (Athlone Press, 1970), 118). But, for all his criticisms of our behaviour, he thought it 'the first condition of sanity' to believe that 'our civilisation is founded in common sense' ('Essay on Comedy', 446).
13. Though less acerbic than the caricaturist Lady Comper in the short story 'The Case of General Ople and Lady Comper'.
14. This marks out the Malvolio in Willoughby: cf. Tinman in the 'House on the Beach', another short story of this period, who dons court clothes and practises bowing in front of a large looking-glass in preparation for a visit to court. Meredith enjoyed reading the part of Malvolio in private play-readings, 'the words of which he trolled forth in the gayest, more infectious manner'. See Lady Butcher's *Memories of George Meredith, OM* (Constable, 1919), 29.
15. Beer suggests that he is, in fact, 'invoking the conventions of the stage, and particularly of Molière's comedies' (*Meredith: A Change of Masks*, 123). There is also something of Peacock here, in the gathering of guests at a country house for purpose of satire, with pairings-off at the end (there are nine brides and bridegrooms at the end of Peacock's last novel of 1860/1, *Gryll Grange*). N.B., Sir Willoughby Patterne's name is symbolic, as Peacock's names are. The reference here is not only to the willow pattern in china, but to his being the very 'pattern' of a country gentleman ('a splendid young representative island lord', 4; 22).
16. Remember, though, that in first passing over Laetitia for a more robust partner he had set aside a 'personal inclination' for her (*E* 3; 16). Also in support of a happy ending, even for Willoughby, there is yet another hint in his name: willows bend rather than break. Moreover, Laetitia like Clara has a poetic nature. Even with her new tougher stance, she is likely to make a good wife.
17. The idea of a needed variation to Pattern(e) fits well with Darwin's

belief in cross-breeding, showing how Meredith has assimilated current scientific ideas into his positive view of life. In *Darwin's Plots: Evolutionary Narratives in Darwin, George Eliot and Nineteenth-Century Fiction* (Cambridge: Cambridge University Press, 2009, 3rd ed.), 94, Beer says, 'It would be easy to make either an optimistic or a pessimistic selection from *The Origin*'. On the whole and predictably, Meredith takes out for himself what is optimistic. But Jonathan Smith argues convincingly that he does take into account the danger of reversion in such cases. See 'The Cock of Lordly Plume': Sexual Selection and *The Egoist*' in *Nineteenth-Century Literature* 50/1 (June 1995): 57–8.

18. According to Kelvin in *A Troubled Eden*, 14, Meredith's Tory leanings never 'actually ceased', but Lady Butcher writes, 'I do not think Mr Meredith liked the company of very rich people', recalling him saying that 'in many cases the vision of rich people was limited to their personal possessions, and that their mental horizon was bounded by their own park gates' (p. 7). This neatly sums up Willoughby's limitations, and his 'grand hereditary desire to transmit his estates, wealth and name to a solid posterity' (23; 192). The whole range of china imagery may have been inspired by the proximity to the Merediths in Surrey of the Wedgwood family. Josiah Wedgwood III (1795–1880), who had married Darwin's sister, retired from the potteries in 1842 and settled at Leith Hill Place a few miles from Box Hill. Meredith never mentions the family and refers only glancingly to Darwin, who often came to visit the Wedgwoods and conducted some of his experiments at their house.

CHAPTER 5. THE LATER NOVELS: MEREDITH AS FEMINIST?

1. Susan Morgan, *Sisters in Time: Imagining Gender in Nineteenth-Century British Fiction* (Oxford: Oxford University Press, 1989), 164.
2. See Leonée Ormond's '*The Tragic Comedians*: Meredith's Use of Image Patterns', Ian Fletcher, ed., *Meredith Now: Some Critical Essays* (Routledge & Kegan Paul, 1971), 238.
3. Beer believes Meredith himself undergoes 'a process of disillusionment with Clotilde' as the narrative progresses (*Meredith: A Change of Masks: A Study of the Novels* (Athlone Press, 1970), 138).
4 Siegfried Sassoon, *Meredith* (Grey Arrow, 1959), 190. D. H. Lawrence's equally revealing verdict on the novel was that it is 'wonderfully clever', but 'too turgid'. *Letters of D. H. Lawrence*, ed. James T. Boulton, Vol. I (Cambridge: Cambridge University Press, 1979), 250.
5. 'I felt that she was in me as I wrote', wrote Meredith (*SL*, 197). He

certainly endows Diana with his own characteristics as a writer. Like him, she 'thought in flashes' but 'wrote...laboriously. The desire to prune, compress, overcharge was a torment', especially to one 'writing under a sharp necessity for payment' (1; 11).
6. See Katherine Frank's *Lucie Duff Gordon: A Passage to Egypt* (Hamish Hamilton, 1994), 116–17.
7. Trollope's novel about a pathologically suspicious husband was one of his highest earning titles, second only (with *Phineas Finn*) to *Can You Forgive Her?* See his *Autobiography* (Penguin, 1993), 332. Caroline Norton's story was still in the public eye even now, thanks to the 1884 amendment to the Married Women's Property Act.
8. This seventeenth-century listed building is on the corner of Raikes Lane and the Guildford Road in Surrey, not far from Box Hill.
9. In *Women and Marriage in Victorian Fiction* (Thames & Hudson, 1976), 193, Jenni Calder sees his pursuit of Diana as more 'forceful' than Vernon's of Clara Middleton. Beer feels that emphasis shifts from the second part of his name to the first, noting that he proposes to Diana 'in the glow of sunset'. She finds him altogether too much of a cipher (*A Change of Masks*, 165); but Meredith's main concern here is with the processes of Diana's mind. Emma too is important, in her physical closeness to Diana serving not just as Redwood's advocate but as his proxy.
10. Anna Maria Jones's criticism in *Problem Novels: Victorian Fiction Theorizes the Sensational Self* (Columbus: Ohio State University, 2007), 125.
11. One has to agree here with Anna Maria Jones, ibid. 23, on Emma's 'eugenicist solicitude' for Diana and Redworth. N.B. in 1908 Meredith wrote to Alice Meynell's daughter Monica that 'Mr Francis Galton bears a name welcome in every English household' (*Letters* III: 173). Eugenics did not have a bad name then.
12. Barbara Hardy, '*Lord Ormont and His Aminta* and *The Amazing Marriage*' in Fletcher, ed., *Meredith Now*, 297.
13. e.g., against the Jews. Meredith's own attitude towards Jews is ambivalent. He often decries Jewish profiteers, and was against Zionism – but only because 'I would have the strong Jewish blood mix with ours', as he told Lucien Wolf in 1909 (*Letters* III: 1551).
14. See Renate Muendel, *George Meredith* (Boston: Twayne, 1986), 114–15, and Beer, *A Change of Masks*, 184. Beer points out the importance of music and silence in the novel. Here more than anywhere one sees what Meredith meant by saying that 'Everything I do is an Experiment' (*Letters* 1: 32).
15. Calder in *Women and Marriage* calls it 'the oddest of Meredith's plots' (p. 193), which is saying a great deal!
16. See Anne C. Henry's '"Explorations in Dot-and-Dashland": George

Meredith's Aphasia', *Nineteenth-Century Literature* 61/3 (December 2006): 311–42.
17. *Recollections*, Vol I (New York: Macmillan, 1917), 47. It was Morley who first introduced Meredith to John Stuart Mill's *On the Subjection of Women*, and who reported his enthusiasm for it (p. 14–15).

CHAPTER 6. THE LATER POETRY

1. Can it be a coincidence that Gallimard brought out a new edition of this in Paris, just after the signing of the Munich Agreement in 1938?
2. George Macbeth, ed., *The Penguin Book of Victorian Verse* (Penguin, 1969), 178.
3. *Meredith* (Grey Arrow, 1959), 237.
4. Graham Hough, in his introduction to *Selected Poems of George Meredith* (Oxford University Press, 1962), 3.
5. 'Sorting and Sifting Meredith's Poetry' in Richard A. Levine, ed., *The Victorian Experience: Poets* (Athens, Oh.: Ohio University Press, 1982), 119. See also John Lucas, 'Meredith as Poet' in Ian Fletcher, ed., *Meredith Now: Some Critical Essays* (Routledge & Kegan Paul, 1971), 15.
6. In *Evolution and Poetic Belief: A Study in Some Victorian and Modern Writers* (Oslo: Oslo University Press, 1956) Roppen emphasizes the personal element: 'it is in the poems, more freely than in his novels, that Meredith confesses himself' (p. 211). On the poetry as 'a participatory environment', see Nicholas Frankel's 'The Textual Environment of George Meredith', *Romanticism and Victorianism on the Net*, No. 47 (August 2007), 11.
7. See *The Poems of George Meredith* II ed. Phyllis Bartlett (New York: Yale University Press, 1978), 207.
8. e.g., consider 'the dark sexual antagonisms, the compulsions to hurt others, the self-destructiveness' in 'Modern Love'. See Carol L. Bernstein's *Precarious Enchantment: A Reading of Meredith's Poetry* (Washington DC: Catholic University Of America, 1979), 23.
9. Perhaps the nearest Meredith gets to embodying this in the novels is in the 'Chief' in *Vittoria*, with his expansive presence and his 'orbed mind' (*V* II; 9).
10. See Patricia Crunden on this process, in 'The Woods of Westermain', *Victorian Poetry* 5/4 (Winter 1967): 265–82, 268.
11. G. M. Trevelyan, *The Poetry and Philosophy of George Meredith* (Constable, 1906), 82.
12. N.B. A different choice from that made in 'Lights Out', by Frost's friend Edward Thomas. John Holmes also plays Meredith's poem

off against Frost's, suggesting that Meredith's woods are primarily emblematic of reality, though, of course, death is a part of that. Meredith chooses to confront *both* with 'Foresight and Patience' rather than try to evade them. Holmes discusses this poem at length in *Darwin's Bards: British and American Poetry in the Age of Evolution* (Edinburgh: Edinburgh University Press, 2009), 107–16.

13. Or, as Holmes puts it, Meredith has moved from a 'synchronic reading emphasizing natural processes happening at the same time to a diachronic reading emphasizing change over time' (ibid. 61). This is a valuable corrective to the idea that Meredith's views on evolution never change.
14. This part is printed in Bartlett's 'Supplementary Textual Notes', *Poems* II, 1183–5.
15. *Letters of D. H. Lawrence,* ed. James T. Boulton (Cambridge: Cambridge University Press, 1979), I: 214, 241.
16. See Mark Osteen's 'Meredith/Joyce: Bella Mount and Bella's Mount', *James Joyce Quarterly* 35/6 (Summer–Fall, 1998): 873–8. For Meredith's more general impact on Joyce, see Richard C. Stevenson, *The Experimental Impulse in George Meredith's Fiction* (Lewisburg, Penn.: Bucknell University Press, 2004), 191–3.
17. See 'Discoveries', *Collected Works of W. B. Yeats* (Stratford: Shakespeare Head, 1908), 10.
18. See Richard Aldington's *Ezra Pound and T. S. Eliot* (The Peacock's Press, 1954), 14. Eliot uses the line ambiguously in his poem. The age of Emerson and Arnold, and Meredith too, has passed, but do they not still stand for timeless values?

Select Bibliography

PRINCIPAL WORKS BY GEORGE MEREDITH

The following section gives the original publisher and date of publication of each novel, its volume number in the Memorial Edition (British Library Shelfmark, 2344.c–d), and any recent editions still likely to be available. Unless otherwise stated, the place of publication is London. Note that Scribner's Memorial Edition has now been scanned into the Internet Archive. There is also a complete edition of *The Works of George Meredith*, arranged by David Widger, with 'Modern Love' in Volume 1 of the poetry, on Project Gutenberg. For these and other internet resources, see <http://www.victorianweb.org/authors/meredith/related.html>.

Novels and Novellas (in chronological order of original publication)

The Shaving of Shagpat: An Arabian Entertainment (Chapman & Hall, 1856 [1855]). Vol. 1.

Farina: A Legend of Cologne (Smith, Elder, 1857). Vol. 21.

The Ordeal of Richard Feverel: A History of Father and Son (Chapman & Hall, 1859). Vol. 2. Ed. C. L. Cline (Boston: Riverside, 1971); ed. John Halperin (Oxford: OUP, World's Classics, 1984); ed. Edward Mendelson (Penguin Classics, 1998).

Evan Harrington: A Novel (New York: Harper & Bros., 1860). Vol. 6.

Emilia in England, later *Sandra Belloni* (Chapman & Hall, 1864). Vols. 3–4.

Rhoda Fleming: A Story (Tinsley Brothers, 1865). Vol. 5.

Vittoria (Chapman & Hall, 1866). Vols. 7–8.

The Adventures of Harry Richmond (Smith, Elder, 1871). Vols. 9–10.

Beauchamp's Career (Chapman & Hall, 1876). Vols. 11–12.

'The House on the Beach: A Realistic Tale', *New Quarterly Magazine* (January 1877). Vol. 22.

'The Case of General Ople and Lady Camper', *New Quarterly Magazine* (July 1877). Vol. 21.
The Egoist: A Comedy in Narrative (Kegan Paul, 1879). Vols. 13–14. Ed. Robert M. Adams, *An Annotated Text, Backgrounds, Criticism*. A Norton Critical Edition (New York: Norton, 1979); ed. George Woodcock (Harmondsworth: Penguin, 2007).
The Tragic Comedians: A Study in a Well-Known Story (Chapman & Hall, 1880). Vol. 15.
Diana of the Crossways: A Novel (Chapman & Hall, 1885). Vol. 16.
One of Our Conquerors (Chapman & Hall, 1891). Vol. 17.
Lord Ormont and his Aminta: A Novel (Chapman & Hall, 1894). Vol. 18.
The Amazing Marriage (Constable, 1895). Vol. 19.
Celt and Saxon (Constable, 1910). Vol. 20.

Poems

The Poems of George Meredith, ed. Phyllis Bartlett. 2 vols. (New York: Yale University Press, 1978). Standard text.
Selected Poems of George Meredith, ed. Graham Hough (Oxford University Press, 1962).
George Meredith: Selected Poems, ed. Keith Hanley (Manchester: Fyfield Books (Carcanet), 1988). More usefully annotated than Hough's.

Essays

'On the Idea of Comedy and the Uses of the Comic Spirit', *New Quarterly Magazine* (April 1877). With miscellaneous prose, such as articles, reviews and journalism, in the Memorial Edition Vol. 23. With annotations by the editor, in *The Egoist, An Annotated Text, Backgrounds, Criticism*. A Norton Critical Edition ed. Robert M. Adams (NewYork: Norton, 1979).

Correspondence

Letters, ed. William M. Meredith, 2 vols. Vol. 1, *1844–1881*; Vol 2, *1882-1909* (Constable, 1912).
Letters, ed. C. L. Cline, 3 vols. Useful biographies of Meredith's correspondents at the end of Vol. 3: 1722–9 (Oxford: Clarendon, 1970).
Selected Letters, ed. Mohammad Shaheen (Macmillan, 1997). Extra letters, not a selection from Cline.
Joukovsky, Nicholas, and Jim Powell. 'A Peacock in the Attic: Insights and Secrets from Newly Discovered Letters by George Meredith'. *Times Literary Supplement*, 22 July 2011, 13–15. Seven uncollected

letters, written 1854–1861, showing Meredith's state of mind in these difficult years.

Bibliographies

Beer, Gillian. 'George Meredith'. George H. Ford, ed., *Victorian Fiction: A Second Guide to Research* (New York: Modern Language Association, 1978), 274–87.
Cline, C. L. 'George Meredith'. Lionel Stevenson, ed., *Victorian Fiction: A Guide to Research* (Cambridge, Mass.: Harvard University Press, 1964), 324–48.
Collie, Michael. *George Meredith: A Bibliography* (Dawson, 1974).
Esdaile, Arundell. *A Chronological List of George Meredith's Publications, 1849–1911* (Walter T. Spencer, 1907).
Olmstedt, John Charles. *George Meredith: An Annotated Bibliography of Criticism, 1925–1975* (New York: Garland, 1978).

BIOGRAPHICAL AND CRITICAL STUDIES

Adams, Robert M., ed. *The Egoist: An Annotated Text, Backgrounds, Criticism*. A Norton Critical Edition (New York: Norton, 1979). Includes 'An Essay on Comedy' and key essays on the novel.
Armstrong, Isobel. *Victorian Poetry: Poetry, Poetics and Politics* (Routledge, 1993). See Chapter 15 on 'Meredith and Others: Hard, Gem-like Dissidence'. Particularly good on 'Modern Love'.
Banerjee, Jacqueline. '"A Game of Cross-Purposes": Letters in George Meredith's *The Ordeal of Richard Feverel*', *English Studies* 92/1 (February 2011): 39–54.
Banfield, Marie. 'Meredith, Mazzini and the *Risorgimento*: The Italian Novels'. *RSV* (*Revista di Studi Vittoriani* 10/21 (January 2006): 57–74). Good discussion of the interwoven evolutionary and revolutionary concerns of the two novels.
Bartlett, Phyllis. *George Meredith* (Longman's, Green & Co. for the British Council, 1963). Still useful, especially on the poetry.
Beer, Gillian. *Meredith: A Change of Masks: A Study of the Novels* (Athlone Press, 1970). Seminal, revealing aspects of Meredith that chime with more recent expectations of the novels.
Bernstein, Carol L. *Precarious Enchantment: A Reading of Meredith's Poetry* (Washington DC: Catholic University of America, 1979). Sees Meredith transcending the conflict between human needs and the 'tidal world' through 'an imaginative act' (p. 171). Helpful though brief links back to Walter Pater.

Butcher, Alice Mary Brandreth, Lady. *Memories of George Meredith, OM* (Constable, 1919). Unique vignettes of Meredith in company.

Calder, Jenni. *Women and Marriage in Victorian Fiction* (Thames & Hudson, 1976). Discussion of *The Egoist* excerpted in Adams, *The Egoist*, 472–80. Praises Meredith for his support of women.

Cline, C. L. 'The Betrothal of George Meredith to Marie Vulliamy', *Nineteenth-Century Fiction* 16/3 (December 1961): 231–43.

Collie, Michael. '"Davy-Lamp Down Below": A Note on *The Amazing Marriage*.' *The Year Book of English Studies* 8 (1978): 249–61. Deals with Meredith's psychological 'diggings and explorings' (p. 249).

Cosslett, Tess. *The 'Scientific Movement' and Victorian Literature* (New York: St Martin's, 1983). See Chapter 4 on Meredith's poetry (pp. 101–31).

Crunden, Patricia. 'The Woods of Westermain'. *Victorian Poetry* 5/4 (Winter 1967): 265–82. Useful close commentary.

Ellis, S. M. *George Meredith: His Life and Friends in Relation to His Work* (Grant Richards, 1920, 2nd ed.). Illuminating firsthand accounts of Meredith by a distant cousin.

Fletcher, Ian, ed. *Meredith Now: Some Critical Essays* (Routledge & Kegan Paul, 1971). Wide-ranging, including essays on the Italian novels, *Rhoda Fleming* etc.

Fletcher, Pauline. 'Trifles Light as Air' in Meredith's *Modern Love*, *Victoria Poetry* 34/1 (Spring 1966): 87–99. The husband seen as a largely unreliable narrator – Othello to his wife's Desdemona.

Frankel, Nicholas. 'The Textual Environment of George Meredith'. *Romanticism and Victorianism on the Net*, No. 47 (August 2007). <http://www.erudit.org/revue/ravon/2007/v/n47/016702ar.html> Robust defence of 'The Woods of Westermain' as a 'textual event' in which we are invited to take part.

Friedman, Norman. 'The Jangled Harp: Symbolic Structure in *Modern Love*'. *Modern Language Quarterly* 18 (1957): 9–26. Focuses on image-clusters.

Hanley, Keith. Introduction and Notes to *George Meredith: Selected Poems*, ed. Hanley (Manchester: Fyfield Books (Carcanet), 1988), 7–24; 101–18. Succinctly analyses Meredith's aims and impact as a poet.

Hardy, Barbara. '*Lord Ormont and His Aminta* and *The Amazing Marriage*' in Fletcher, *Meredith Now*, 295–312. Sensitive appreciation, especially of the deeper and more truly 'pastoral' *Amazing Marriage* (p. 304).

———, 'The Structure of Imagery: George Meredith's *Harry Richmond*'. *The Appropriate Form* (Athlone Press, 1964), 83–104. Allows for 'casual and wayward richness' in the imagery (p. 104), much the best approach to it.

Harman, Barbara Leah. *The Feminine Political Novel in Victorian England* (Charlottesville, VA: University Press of Virginia, 1998). A fine chapter on *Diana*, Meredith's connection with the feminist poet Louisa Shore, his 'critique of chivalry' (p. 80), etc .

Harris, Margaret. Introduction, *Beauchamp's Career* (Oxford: Oxford University Press, World's Classics, 1988), vii–xxviii. Contextualizes the novel politically and ideologically, and analyses the women's roles, particularly Jenny's.

———, 'George Meredith at the Crossways' in William Baker and Kenneth Womack, eds, *A Companion to the Victorian Novel* (Greenwood, 2002), 341–52. Inspiring round-up of new approaches.

Harris, Wendell. 'Sorting and Sifting Meredith's Poetry' in Richard A. Levine, ed., *The Victorian Experience: Poets* (Athens, Oh.: Ohio University Press, 1982), 115–37. Recommends strict selectivity.

Henry, Anne C. '"Explorations in Dot-and-Dashland": George Meredith's Aphasia', *Nineteenth-Century Literature* 61/3 (December 2006): 311–42. Examines Meredith's 'fascination with the unarticulated and inarticulate' (Headnote, p. 311).

Hill, Charles J. 'The Portrait of the Author in *Beauchamp's Career*'. *Journal of English and Germanic Philology* 52/3 (July 1953): 332–9. Useful on Meredith's anti-clericalism (from which Jessopp and others were exempt) and his attitude to prayer and divinity.

Holmes, John. *Darwin's Bards: British and American Poetry in the Age of Evolution* (Edinburgh: Edinburgh University Press, 2009). Skilfully traces the development as well as the various strands of Meredith's evolutionary thinking in several of his key poems.

Hough, Graham. Introduction, *Selected Poems of George Meredith* (Oxford: Oxford University Press, 1962), 1–17. Emphasizes Meredith's adventurousness, frankness, vitalism.

Howard, David. 'George Meredith: "Delicate" and "Epical" Fiction' in John Lucas, ed., *Literature and Politics in the Nineteenth Century* (Methuen, 1971), 131–71. Focuses on the Italian novels (showing their relevance to the English situation too) and *Beauchamp's Career*, placing it above *The Egoist* in 'fullness...resonance...ambition' (p. 160).

Jones, Anna Maria. *Problem Novels: Victorian Fiction Theorizes the Sensational Self* (Columbus: Ohio State University Press, 2007). Well-contextualized discussions of *Diana* and *The Egoist* in Chapter 3.

Jones, Mervyn. *The Amazing Victorian: A Life of George Meredith* (Constable, 1999). A good all-round literary biography though the plot summaries at the end are not always dependable (e.g. that of *Richard Feverel* is not complete, and Flitch in *The Egoist* is not dismissed for drunkenness).

Karl, Frederick R. '*Beauchamp's Career*: An English Ordeal', *Nineteenth-Century Fiction* 16/2 (September 1961): 117–31. Ranks the novel highly in the *oeuvre* but still reads it negatively.

Kelvin, Norman. *A Troubled Eden: Nature and Society in the Works of George Meredith* (Stanford: Stanford University Press, 1968). Shows how eclectically Meredith belonged to his times, and how his various convictions co-existed 'within the controlling forms of his art' (p. 4).

Lindsay, Jack. *George Meredith: His Life and Work* (Bodley Head, 1956). Thoroughgoing Marxist approach: sees Meredith wishing for union with nature as a stepping-stone to 'union with his oppressed fellows' (p. 34).

Lucas, John. 'Meredith as Poet' in Fletcher, *Meredith Now*, 14–33. Sees 'Modern Love' as the 'one undoubted major triumph' of his poetry (p. 22).

———, 'Meredith's Reputation' in Adams, ed., *The Egoist*, 539–51.

Lund, Michael. 'Space and Spiritual Crisis in Meredith's "Modern Love"'. *Victorian Poetry* 16/4 (Winter 1978): 376–82. Shows the wider questioning provoked by the marriage breakdown.

Manos, Nikki Lee. Introduction, *Diana of the Crossways: A Novel* (Detroit: Wayne State University Press, 2001), 7–30. Update on critical approaches, with useful bibliography.

Mermin, Dorothy M. 'Poetry as Fiction: Meredith's *Modern Love*', *ELH* 43/1 (1976): 100–19. Explores 'novelistic' elements in the sonnets (p. 100).

Mendelson, Edward. Introduction to *The Ordeal of Richard Feverel* (Penguin Classics, 1998), xi–xxx. Useful on the different editions of the novel, and what they suggest.

Morgan, Susan. *Sisters in Time: Imagining Gender in Nineteenth-Century British Fiction* (Oxford: Oxford University Press, 1989). Chapter 6 draws out the tensions in Meredith's presentation of his heroines.

Muendel, Renate. *George Meredith* (Boston: Twayne, 1986). Sympathetic to Meredith's 'lifelong attempt to join romance and realism in a paradoxical and precarious balance' (p. 124), as well as to his 'large, vigorous spirit' (p. 130).

Payne, Susan. *Difficult Discourse: George Meredith's Experimental Fiction* (Pisa: ETS, 1995). Stimulating; shows Meredith's 'critical stance before realist techniques and conventions' (p. 62).

Pulford, J. S. L. *George & Mary Meredith in Weybridge, Shepperton & Esher 1849–61*. Walton & Weybridge Local History Society: Paper No. 27 (1989). Well-researched paper on Meredith's early years and first marriage.

Reader, Willie D. 'The Autobiographical Author as Fictional Character: Point of View in Meredith's "Modern Love"'. *Victorian Poetry* 10/2 (Summer 1972): 131–43.

Roberts, Neil. *Meredith and the Novel* (Macmillan, 1997). Bakhtinian approach exactly suited to the novels' 'conflict-ridden linguistic diversity' (p. 2).

Rodenbeck, John von B. 'The Classicism of Meredith's "Love in the Valley"'. *Victorian Poetry* 11/1 (Spring 1973): 27–37. Shows classical influence permeating the poem.

Roppen, Georg. *Evolution and Poetic Belief: A Study in Some Victorian and Modern Writers* (Oslo: Oslo University Press, 1956). Sympathetic to Meredith's 'self-effacing and heroic agnosticism' (p. 278), whilst suggesting the ultimate inadequacy of his vision. See Chapter 3, Part 2.

Sassoon, Siegfried. *Meredith* (Grey Arrow, 1959). Often critically revealing, despite the admiring stance.

Shuttleworth, Sally. *The Mind of the Child: Child Development in Literature, Science, and Medicine, 1830–1900* (Oxford: Oxford University Press, 2010). Excellent close analysis of the earlier chapters of *Feverel* and their outcome, placing Meredith on the threshold of new developments in 'the science of child study' (p. 178).

Smith, Jonathan. '"The Cock of Lordly Plume": Sexual Selection and *The Egoist*'. *Nineteenth-Century Literature* 50/1 (June 1995): 51–77. Shows Meredith applying the corrective of the comic spirit to Darwin as well as Willoughby.

Soccio, Anna Enrichetta, ed., *Beauchamp's Career: George Meredith: Testo e Contesto*. (Rome: Aracne, 2008). Confirms the inexhaustibility of just one Meredith novel: a variety of new approaches, many in English, by Banfield, Payne, Roberts and others.

Stevenson, Lionel. *Darwin Among the Poets* (Chicago: Chicago University Press, 1932). Pioneering full-length study on this subject; see Chapter 4 on Meredith.

⸺, *The Ordeal of George Meredith* (Peter Owen, 1954). Helpful biography still, despite gaps and lack of notes.

Stevenson, Richard C. *The Experimental Impulse in George Meredith's Fiction* (Lewisburg, Penn.: Bucknell University Press, 2004). Discusses Meredith as a forerunner of the modernists.

Stone, James S. *George Meredith's Politics: As Seen in his Life, Friendships and Works* (Oakville, Ont.: P. D. Meany, 1986). Balanced view of Meredith as a 'writer' rather than 'righter' of injustices, who points to moral imperatives and 'eternal interests' (p. 164).

Trevelyan, G. M. *The Poetry and Philosophy of George Meredith* (Constable, 1906). The classic study, fully cognisant of, but undeterred by, Meredith's difficulty as a poet.

White, Allon. *The Uses of Obscurity: The Fiction of Early Modernism* (Routledge & Kegan Paul, 1981). Stimulating discussion of 'antagonistic voices' in the narratives (p. 49).

Williams, Carolyn. 'Natural Selection and Narrative Form in *The Egoist'*. *Victorian Studies* 27/1 (Autumn 1983): 53–79. Shows Meredith's irony directed against misinterpretations of evolutionary theory rather than the theory itself.

Williams, David. *George Meredith: His Life and Lost Love* (Hamish Hamilton, 1977). Entertaining but sometimes speculative; no scholarly references.

Williams, Ioan, ed. *Meredith: The Critical Heritage* (Routledge & Kegan Paul, 1971). Invaluable for tracing Meredith's reception up to 1911.

Wilt, Judith. *The Readable People of George Meredith* (Princeton: Princeton University Press, 1975). Pioneering work on Meredith and the 'real and the fictional reader' (p. 4).

Wolf, Lynn E. 'A Bracing Corrective: Women and Comedy in George Meredith's "Case of General Ople and Lady Camper"'. *Essays in Literature* 1 (1994). Available at <http://www.accessmylibrary.com/article-1G1-16082467/bracing-corrective-women-and.html>. Close analysis with useful connections to the *oeuvre*.

Woolf, Virginia. 'The Novels of George Meredith', rpt. Adams, ed., *The Egoist*, 531–9. Responds to Meredith's uniqueness, originality and verve, but finds 'his teaching...too insistent' (p. 538).

BACKGROUND READING

Beer, Gillian. *Darwin's Plots: Evolutionary Narratives in Darwin, George Eliot and Nineteenth-Century Fiction* (Cambridge: Cambridge University Press, 2009, 3rd ed.). See especially Chapter 7, 'Descent and Sexual Selection: Women in Narrative' (pp. 196–219).

Cosslett, Tess. Introduction, *Science and Religion in the Nineteenth Century* (Cambridge: Cambridge University Press, 1984): 1–24.

Halperin, John. *Egoism and Self-Discovery in the Victorian Novel: Studies in the Ordeal of Knowledge in the Nineteenth Century* (New York: Burt Franklin, 1974). Useful context for Meredith's main preoccupation (also discusses Meredith himself).

Hardman, William. *A Mid-Victorian Pepys: The Letters and Memoirs of Sir William Hardman, MA FRGS*. ed. S. M. Ellis (Cecil Palmer, 1923). Memoirs of Meredith's close friend.

Joukovsky, Nicholas. 'New Correspondence of Mary Ellen Meredith'. *Studies in Philology* 106/4 (Fall 2009): 483–522. Gives more insights into Meredith's first marriage.

Keating, Peter. *The Haunted Study: A Social History of the English Novel, 1875–1914* (Secker & Warburg, 1989). See Chapter 7, 'Readers and Novelists'.

Knoepflmacher, U. C. *Nature and the Victorian Imagination* (Berkeley: University of California Press, 1978).

Morley, John. *Recollections*, Vols. I and II (New York: Macmillan, 1917).
O'Gorman, Francis. *The Victorian Novel: A Guide to Criticism* (Oxford: Blackwell, 2002).
Rylance, Rick. *Victorian Psychology and British Culture, 1850–1880* (Oxford: Oxford University Press, 2000).

Index

Aldington, Richard, 112
Armstrong, Isobel, 103
Arnold, Matthew, 112

Banfield, Marie, 105, 106, 107
Barrie, James, 19, 20, 103
Bartlett, Phyllis, 103, 104, 111, 112
Beer, Gillian, 31, 104, 106, 108, 109, 110
Bernstein, Carol L., 111
Brontë, Anne, 105
Brontë, Charlotte, 82
Browning, Robert, 19, 27
Bulwer-Lytton, Edward, 9
Burne-Jones, Philip (son of Edward Burne-Jones), 20
Butcher, Alice Mary Brandreth, Lady (friend), 108, 109
Butler, A. J. (reviewer), 59

Calder, Jenni, 110
Carlyle, Thomas, 60, 106, 107
Cervantes, Miguel de, 65, 66
Chapman and Hall (publishers), 14, 18, 40, 41, 53, 59
Charnock, Richard (solicitor), 7
Chatterton, Thomas, 13
Cline, C. L., 102
Clodd, Edward (friend), 22
Comte, Auguste, 2, 101, 107
Conan Doyle, Arthur, 19, 20, 99
Constable (publishers), 102, 105, 107, 108, 111
Conway, Moncure, 62

Cornhill Magazine, The, 57, 59
Courteney, W. L. (editor), 81
Crane, Walter (artist), 40
Crimea, 28, 60
Crunden, Patricia, 111

Darwin, Charles, 2, 19, 43, 49, 64, 75, 107, 108–9, 112
Dickens, Charles, 48, 55
Dönniges, Hélène von, 77
Duff Gordon, Sir Alexander, 10, 16, 39
Duff Gordon, Janet (later Mrs Ross), 10, 49, 50
Duff Gordon, Lady Lucie, 79, 110

Edward VII, King, 20, 102
Ellis, S. M. (second cousin), 101, 102, 103, 106
Eliot, George, 40, 82, 109
Eliot, T. S., 99, 112

Fielding, Henry, 65
Fortnightly Review, The, 8, 18, 19, 81
Frank, Katherine (biographer), 110
Frankel, Nicholas, 111
Friedman, Norman, 104
Frith, William (artist), 9
Frost, Robert, 96, 11, 112

Galton, Sir Francis (eugenicist), 110

Goldsmith, Oliver, 65

Haggard, Rider, 20
Hanley, Keith, 92
Hardman, William (friend), 14, 17, 20, 24, 42, 58, 103
Hardy, Barbara, 106, 107, 110
Hardy, Thomas (novelist), 19, 20, 99, 100
Hardy, Thomas, Sir (Rear Admiral), 101
Harris, Margaret, 108
Harris, Wendell, 92, 103
Hearn, Lafcadio, 101
Hearne, Edward (physician), 108
Henry, Anne C., 110
Hill, Charles J., 108
Holman Hunt, William (artist) and Edith, 20
Holmes, John, 111, 112
Horne, Catherine (wife of Richard Horne), 12
Horne, Richard Hengist (poet, critic etc.), 22, 27
Hough, Graham, 92, 111
Howard, David, 105, 106, 108

James, Henry, 19, 20
Jessopp, Reverend Augustus, 16, 39, 52
Jones, Anna Marie, 110
Jones, Mervyn (biographer), 102, 105, 107
Joukovsky, Nicholas (biographer), 102
Joyce, James, 99, 112

Karl, Frederick, 107
Kelvin, Norman, 107, 109
Kingsley, Charles, 55
Kipling, Rudyard, 20

Lasalle, Ferdinand, 77
Lawrence, D. H., 99, 109, 112

Lewes, G. H., 2
Lindsay, Jack, 107
Lund, Michael, 104

MacBeth, George, 91, 111
Maceroni, Elizabeth, 9, 11
Maceroni, Emilie, 11, 16, 51
Macpherson, James, 26
Mansfield, Charles (scientist), 11, 104
Maxse, Admiral Frederick (friend), 2, 14, 16, 17, 20, 29, 52, 60, 62, 101, 107
Mayo, Robert D., 75
Mazzini, Guiseppe (Italian nationalist), 52, 106
Melbourne, Lord, 79
Mendelson, Edward, 102, 105
Meredith, Arthur (first son), 11, 13, 14, 16, 20, 26, 42
Meredith, Augustus (father), 5, 6, 7
Meredith, George
   Ideas and themes:
      Comic Spirit, the, 65–8, 70, 73, 98, 108
      egoism, 7, 34, 40, 44, 68–74, 77, 84, 85, 88, 85, 93–4
      eugenics, 110
      evolution, 2, 19, 49, 75, 83, 90, 93–4, 96, 102, 105, 107, 109, 111, 112
      feminism, 2, 19, 67–8, 76, 78–83, 85–90, 101
      heroism, 39–41, 46, 57, 59–65, 68–74, 77, 82, 83–4, 86, 95, 106–7
      Italian uprisings, 17, 46, 52–3
      Jews, 77, 85, 110
      optimism, 27, 70, 99, 103, 109
      pantheism, 102
      Positivism, 2, 102

INDEX

radicalism, 2, 14, 61–5, 85, 101, 107–8, 109
unorthodoxy, 2–3, 7, 10, 20, 63, 83–4, 102
Providence, 43, 48, 50
sentimentalism, 18, 52, 66, 76, 105, 107
Forms and style:
　Bildungsroman, 1, 41, 53, 59, 104
　classicism, 26, 103
　Condition of England novel, 61
　epic, 26, 41, 89, 91, 108
　experimentalism, 3–4, 10, 86, 89, 99, 110
　fantasy, 10, 13, 14, 39–41
　sonnet, 28–38
　style, 3–4, 18, 19, 40, 59, 89
Works:
　Poetry:
　　'Change in Recurrence' 97, 99
　　'Chillianwallah', 8, 12
　　'Daphne', 26, 27
　　'Dirge in Woods', 25, 95–6, 99
　　'France, December 1870', 91
　　'Grandfather Bridgeman', 28
　　'Hymn to Colour', 95
　　'I Chafe at Darkness', 28
　　'In the Woods', 96
　　'Juggling Jerry', 27–8, 89
　　'King Harald's Trance', 91
　　'The Lark Ascending', 95, 100
　　'Love in the Valley', 10, 25, 32, 92, 96, 103
　　'Lucifer in Starlight', 99
　　'Modern Love', 1, 13, 14, 27–38, 41, 42, 48, 59, 78, 91, 92, 101, 102, 103–4, 111
　　'Night of Frost in May', 98
　　'The Nuptials of Attila', 91
　　'Ode to the Spirit of Earth in Autumn', 25, 27, 98, 104
　　'The Old Chartist', 27, 101
　　'Orchard and Heath', 96–7
　　'Pastorals', 24
　　'Pictures of the Rhine', 23
　　'Promise in Disturbance', 37
　　'The Shipwreck of Idomeneus', 26
　　'Song in the Songless', 98, 99
　　'Song ("Love within the Lover's Breast")', 22
　　'Song ("No, no, the falling blossom is no sign")', 27
　　'South-West Wind in the Woodland', 24, 25
　　'A Stave of Roving Time', 25
　　'The Thrush in February', 96
　　'Twilight Music', 23
　　'Wandering Willie', 24
　　'The Woods of Westermain', 2, 20, 36, 92–5, 111
　　'Youth and Age', 20
　Novels, Short Stories and Essay:
　　The Adventures of Harry Richmond, 1–2, 3, 6, 7, 17, 41, 53–8, 59, 63, 97, 105, 106, 107
　　The Amazing Marriage, 19, 52, 88–9
　　Beauchamp's Career, 1, 2, 3, 6, 14, 17, 55, 59–65, 68, 77, 79, 83, 85, 101, 106–8, 113
　　'The Case of General Ople and Lady Camper', 72, 108

INDEX

Celt and Saxon, 89–90, 91
Diana of the Crossways, 1, 2, 3, 18, 19, 20, 26, 66, 78–83, 86, 88, 98, 99, 109–10
The Egoist, 1, 2, 17, 25, 59, 67, 68–75, 76, 77, 99, 101, 103–4, 108–9
Emilia in England (later, *Sandra Belloni*), 16, 17, 48, 51–2, 88
Essay on Comedy and the Uses of the Comic Spirit, 1, 17, 45, 65–8, 108
Evan Harrington, 5, 11, 15, 16, 48, 49–50, 51, 53, 82, 85, 105
Farina, 13, 39–41, 61, 104
'The House on the Beach', 75, 108
Lord Ormont and His Aminta, 6, 19, 86–8, 110
One of Our Conquerors, 3, 19, 83–6
The Ordeal of Richard Feverel, 1, 7, 13, 41–8, 105
Rhoda Fleming, 17, 48, 50–1, 86, 106
The Shaving of Shagpat, 10, 39–40, 41, 72, 99, 104
'The Tale of Chloe', 5, 76–7, 78, 81
The Tragic Comedians, 76, 77–8, 109
Vittoria, 16, 17, 21, 48, 51, 52–3
Meredith, Jane (*née* Macnamara, mother), 5
Meredith, Marie (Mariette, or Riette, daughter), 17
Meredith, Marie (*née* Vulliamy, second wife), 16, 17, 20, 25, 102
Meredith, Mary Ellen (*née* Nicolls, first wife), 9, 11, 12, 13, 15, 16, 20, 23, 24, 28, 42, 49, 102, 107
Meredith, William (second son), 17
Mill, John Stuart, 68
Millais, Sir John Everett, 14, 15
Milner, Lady Violet Georgina (*née* Maxse, friend), 101
Molière (Jean Baptiste Poquelin), 65, 66, 68, 108
Moravian Brothers' School, Neuwidd, 6, 8, 41, 102
Morley, John (editor), 18, 90, 111
Mudie's Lending Library, 51
Muendel, Renate, 106, 110

Norton, Lady Caroline, 1, 78, 79, 83, 110
Nicolls, Edith (step-daughter), 10, 20
Nicolls, Edward (Lieutenant, Mary Ellen Meredith's first husband), 9, 107

Ormond, Leonée, 109

Patmore, Coventry, 29, 35
Pattison, Mark, 22
Payne, Susan, 104
Peacock, Edward (brother-in-law), 8
Peacock, Rosa (sister-in-law), 9
Peacock, Thomas Love (father-in-law), 8, 9, 11, 22, 108
Pulford, J. S. L., 102

Reader, Willie, 104
reputation, Meredith's, 1, 20, 21, 101
Rodenbeck, John von B., 103
Ross, Henry (archaelogist), 15
Rossetti, Dante Gabriel, 14
Rossetti, William Michael, 14
Rousseau, Jean-Jacques, 43

Sandys, Frederick (artist), 16
Sassoon, Siegfried, 7, 8, 59, 91, 102, 105, 106, 107, 109
Scott, A. J. (Professor), 22
Shakespeare, William, 29, 33, 34, 37
Sharp, William (aka Fiona MacLeod), 10, 22, 102
Shuttleworth, Sally, 105
Sidney, Sir Philip, 30
Smith, Jonathan, 109
Spectator, The, 14, 17, 26
Spencer, Herbert (biologist and sociologist), 43, 105
Spenser, Edmund, 32, 37
Stephen, Sir Leslie, 2, 20, 71
Stevenson, Lionel (biographer), 101, 102, 103
Stevenson, Richard C., 106, 112
Stevenson, Robert Louis, 19
Stone, James S., 108
Swinburne, Algernon, 14, 17, 53

Taylor, Tom (editor), 10
Tennyson, Alfred, Lord, 10, 19, 26, 103

Thackeray, William Makepeace, 59
Thompson, Flora, 19, 102
Trevelyan, George Macaulay, 95, 111
Trollope, Anthony, 51, 79, 106, 110

Wallis, Henry (artist), 12, 105
Watts, Mary (widow of G. F. Watts), 20
Wedgwood, Josiah III, 109
White, Allom, 106
Wilde, Oscar, 19, 75
Williams, David, 102, 107
Williams, Ioan, 120
Williams, Ralph Vaughan (composer), 100
Williamson, Francis John (sculptor), 13
Wilt, Judith, 107
Wood, Mrs Henry, 18
Woolf, Virginia, 3, 9, 47, 99
Wordsworth, William, 24, 55

Young England Movement, 107

www.ingramcontent.com/pod-product-compliance
Lightning Source LLC
Chambersburg PA
CBHW051814230426
43672CB00012B/2730